The Design Language of

Timeless East

The Design Language of
Timeless East

WU BIN

New York · Paris · London · Milan

Timeless East

Design, in many eyes, begins with an idea. Concepts unfurl into creations, taking shape as forms, as spaces. But at times, creation begins not in the mind but in the hand—in touch, in the quiet patience of feeling. Such an approach finds particular resonance in Eastern traditions, where a garden is not designed but cultivated through *jingying* (经营), with care and attentiveness. A landscape painting does not pursue scientific composition but follows *xieyi* (写意), a freehand expression that captures spirit more than structure. The artist or garden maker is known as an *yijiang* (意匠), a quiet artisan in whom inner sensibility and form meet in the slow cadence of making. *Timeless East* draws from this lineage. It does not seek to revive the past nor to extend Western modernism; instead, it listens—to time as it lingers and returns, to space as it breathes and remembers. In this view, material is not inert; it holds memory. Proportion is not measurement, but balance felt in the body. *Liubai* (留白), the art of emptiness, gives form to its resonance, just as silence gives shape to sound. A leaf falling, a shadow shifting, the wind brushing through a corridor—each may open a moment outside of time, a kind of timeless time. And in that moment, space becomes more than what is seen. It becomes what is sensed, remembered, and quietly understood.

Shanghai Modern

"The sun had just sunk below the horizon and a gentle breeze caressed one's face. The muddy water of Soochow Creek, transformed to a golden green, flowed quietly westward. The evening tide from the Whangpoo had turned imperceptibly... Faint strains of music were borne on the wind from the park across the river... Under a sunset-mottled sky, the towering framework of Garden Bridge was mantled in a gathering mist. Whenever a tram passed over the bridge, the overhead cable suspended below the top of the steel frame threw off bright, greenish sparks. Looking east, one could see the warehouses on the waterfront of Pootung, like huge monsters crouching in the gloom... To the west, one saw with a shock of wonder on the roof of a building a gigantic neon sign in flaming red and phosphorescent green: LIGHT, HEAT, POWER."

The Shanghai of the 1930s, as depicted in Mao Dun's novel *Midnight*, was undeniably a city brimming with vitality and allure. As the only Chinese metropolis to have completed its first wave of industrialization, urbanization, and globalization in sync with the world, Shanghai has, over the past century, become the epitome of modern life. At one time, the very term "modern" was virtually interchangeable with the city itself. Known as the "Paris of the East," Shanghai not only embraced this cosmopolitan identity but also preserved the profound cultural heritage of Jiangnan, a region located in the lower Yangtze River delta, historically renowned for its wealth and cultural richness. To Shanghai and its inhabitants, "modern" (摩登) signifies more than a contemporary way of life; it embodies an avant-garde spirit that transcends tradition, an ethos of perpetual reinvention, and an infinite horizon of possibilities for both the present and the future.

On one hand, Shanghai, in the throes of modernization, adopted Western amenities such as modern apartments, grand theaters, jazz ballrooms, and racetracks—symbols of its cosmopolitan identity. On the other, the city cultivated a distinctive regional character deeply rooted in its own cultural lineage. The shikumen architecture, calendar posters, and the rise of urban romance novels all reflected a growing national consciousness. Those cultural forms that originated in the West had long since intertwined with indigenous traditions, giving birth to an entirely new artistic aesthetic, architectural vernacular, and unique design philosophy. Today, the Bund's eclectic skyline and the serene elegance of Yu Garden continue to narrate Shanghai's long history of East-West symbiosis.

Shanghai is an enigma, a manifestation of modernity in its own right. Whether viewed from within or from without, through Eastern eyes or Western perspectives, the city never appears the same to any two observers. Just as people find equal delight in the swinging rhythms of Fletcher Henderson's "Shanghai Shuffle" and the cinematic intrigue of Marlene Dietrich in *Shanghai Express*, they are equally drawn to the city's more native rhythms—the casual chatter echoing through the alleyways, the meandering waterways of Yu Garden, and the vibrant, bustling scenes of Chenghuang Temple. Shanghai's modernity has never been static; rather, it is a dynamic force continuously redefined by the collision and convergence of Eastern and Western cultures. More than a fantastical utopia of imagination, Shanghai is a space where modern civilization and classical Eastern heritage intersect, negotiate, and are rewritten.

To grasp the resonance and divergence between Eastern and Western spirits, one could hardly find a better starting point than Shanghai itself.

The Modernity of the East

When modern civilization awakened Asian societies from their pastoral dreams, it also introduced a reverence for efficiency and speed, along with an unrelenting pursuit of greater productivity. Skyscrapers became symbols of modernization. Mountains, temples, and farmlands gradually faded from memory, replaced by overburdened city streets, escalating climate concerns, and an ever-accelerating urban rhythm. In such a modern world, has alienation become the only path forward?

Perhaps, Asia holds another possibility.

Just an hour and a half from Shanghai, Suzhou remains home to over sixty Jiangnan-style classical gardens. Constructed in the compositional spirit of Chinese landscape painting, the youngest of these gardens is nearly 280 years old, while the oldest, Canglang Pavilion, dates back nearly a millennium. The Japanese writer and garden scholar Gotō Asatarō, upon traveling through China, observed that the grandeur of Chinese gardens stemmed from the magnificent artistry of nature itself. He noted that such ambition was beyond Japan's reach and admired the diversity of Chinese gardens, remarking that each had its own character—whether majestic, gentle, pristine, or imbued with Zen—without ever being mere repetitions.

The inspiration that gardens and landscape painting offer to modern spatial design lies in the principle of *yi sui wo dong* (意随我动), "the mind moves as I move," or simply, the alignment of one's thoughts with one's physical motion. In Chinese calligraphy and painting, artists strive for *xin shou xiang ying* (心手相应), a seamless harmony between inner intention and hand movement, allowing the creative process to flow as naturally as drifting clouds and running water. Simultaneously, they seek the state of *wu wo liang wang* (物我两忘), a transcendence of self, where the creator loses awareness of his or her own existence, dissolving into the act of creation itself. Deeply influenced by Daoist *wu wei* (无为, "effortless action") and Zen's *yixin buluan* (一心不乱, "undistracted mind") and *zhizhi renxin* (直指人心, "direct perception of truth"), this philosophy encourages absolute immersion in the present moment, achieving a union with one's craft that defies time itself.

Take, for instance, the practice of *die shi* (叠石), the art of rock arrangement, which is a defining element of scholars' gardens. Rocks sculpted by water erosion, known as *hu shi* (lake stones), are chosen for their porous, intricate forms, reminiscent of the abstract sculptures of Henry Moore and Isamu Noguchi. Arranging these stones is not merely an act of manual labor but a meditative process requiring deep intellectual engagement, no less complex than the meticulous raking of dry sand in a *karesansui*. To stack stones is not simply to imitate mountain forms but to distill their essence, evoking grandeur through deliberate minimalism.

In a Chinese garden, the deliberate empty spaces between the rockeries and the surrounding architectural structures, along with the rocks' own geometric forms, foster a perfect interplay between the visible and the invisible, the tangible and the implied scenes. As garden historian Chen Congzhou suggests in *On Chinese Gardens* (说园), garden-making is a multidisciplinary endeavor that combines the visible elements—such as water, rocks, and pavilions—with the invisible, evoking a poetic and painterly sensibility. The interplay of shadow and light, rain and mist, all contribute to the continuous transformation of the scene. A lake stone, sculpted by time and nature, assumes a dual identity—both natural and crafted—bridging architecture and landscape. Through the art of stacking stones, the relationship among humans, objects, and environment unfolds with clarity, and the scholar's inner world takes physical form, granting the garden an inexhaustible depth and resonance.

Yet the concept *yi sui wo dong* (意随我动) carries another layer of meaning: the mind moves not only through the act of creation—such as in painting, writing, and sculpting—but also through the body's movement within space. The garden-maker alternates between the roles of creator and dweller. The meandering pathways and shifting perspectives of a Chinese garden guide both footsteps and thoughts, blending human intent with natural scenery to craft a richly layered sensory experience. The arrangement of sightlines and routes directs movement and perception, while the fusion of natural and built elements achieves a state of "though man-made, it appears as if nature's gift." In this sense, an ideal spatial composition should embrace the very "core" of the classical garden, as outlined in *A Record of the Gardens of Jiangnan* (江南园林志): first, a harmonious balance between openness and enclosure (第一, 疏密得宜); second, the artful execution of winding paths that guide and reveal (其次, 曲折尽致); and third, a continuous unfolding of framed views and shifting vistas within one's sightline (第三, 眼前有景).

Today, as we inevitably build with modern technologies and materials, it is no longer necessary to construct literal gardens to evoke the spirit of landscape painting and classical garden-making. By internalizing their underlying philosophy and design strategies, we can craft spaces that speak to contemporary Eastern lifestyles and cultural memory. Such designs not only embody the aesthetics of the East but also meet the needs and sensibilities of the present, forging a bridge between past and future.

Timeless East: My Design Language

Space is a medium of communication and, like any medium, it requires a language. This language transcends words and syllables, conveying thought and emotion through light, form, and structure. It speaks to something elemental, as our sense of scale, proportion, and spatial perception is largely intuitive. Yet, this language is far from uniform. It carries regional inflections, shaped by history and culture: the way we construct space reflects not only how we live but how we see and interpret the world.

Unfortunately, Eastern perspectives have often been underrepresented in the narrative of modern design. From the *chinoiserie* of the seventeenth and eighteenth centuries to the *Japonisme* craze of the nineteenth century, what often emerged were not true reflections of the East but stylized projections filtered through Western imagination. Even in the wake of China's rapid economic ascent over the past two decades, this imbalance persists, revealing a deeper absence: the East's authorship in shaping and reimagining its own cultural and artistic language.

So, what exactly constitutes the design language of the modern East? In an age of globalization, how can we move beyond the superficial adoption and admiration of Eastern motifs and visual symbols, and instead ground our expressions in philosophy and perception, articulating a contemporary vision of the "Eastern realm"? I offer an answer through my design language: Timeless East. This is not a stylistic formula or a set of decorative techniques, but rather a philosophical and aesthetic reconstruction—a design ethos rooted in Eastern sensibilities and interwoven with phenomenology, temporality, and the spirit of place. It advocates for a poetic mode of dwelling, guided by embodied experience, addressing the spiritual disconnection of urban life and cultivating a nuanced harmony between human beings, nature, culture, and time.

My design philosophy and aesthetic system have been distilled into eight core principles, collectively known as the "Eight Intentions": "Rationality of Spatial Construction (空间建构的理性)," "Timeless and Precise Proportions (精确隽永的比例)," "Introspective Light and Shadow (勾勒自性的光影)," "Elegant and Refined Details (优雅考究的细部)," "Thresholds Between Spaces (空间之间的间隙)," "Interior-Exterior Dialogue (内外并置的观游)," "Paradoxical Reconstructions (反常合道的重构)," and "Relaxed and Unrestrained Atmosphere (自在松动的日常)." The first four principles emphasize the shared values between Eastern and Western architectural traditions, highlighting structural clarity, precise proportions, and materiality. The latter four, however, delve into a uniquely Eastern spatial logic: a poetics of ambiguity and nuance, a choreography of movement and pause, and an intuition drawn from daily rhythms and literary sensibilities. These intentions emerge from my lived experience, deeply rooted in cultural memory and personal perception.

Specifically, "Thresholds Between Spaces" embodies Eastern philosophical concepts of undifferentiated space and the creative void. As the *Tao Te Ching* expresses, "We make a vessel from a lump of clay, but it is the empty space within the vessel that makes it useful." In design, this *emptiness* is not a mere void but a fertile reservoir of potential, where *qi* (energy) flows and *yi* (intention) unfolds. It is a space of suggestion, subtlety, and resonance. The concept of "undifferentiated space" is akin to the mist among mountains or the blankness in an ink painting. It is a spatial state not yet defined by language or structure—one that exists prior to clearly delineated functions or forms. Like the interplay of void and form in traditional landscape painting, it remains open, undefined, and full of tension. This ambiguity invites greater freedom for imagination and perception, while also allowing the space itself to evolve.

"Interior-Exterior Dialogue" draws inspiration from the integration of wooden architecture and courtyards in Chinese gardens, emphasizing fluid spatial boundaries and a dynamic balance between movement and stillness. Through shifting perspectives, framed views, and compositions that are seemingly discrete yet connected, it creates a temporal spatial experience, echoing Bergson's notion of duration and Song dynasty painter Guo Xi's concept of "walking, viewing, dwelling, and touring."

"Paradoxical Reconstructions," inspired by the poetic logic of Su Shi—an eminent Song dynasty poet, painter, and scholar who famously wrote, "There is painting in poetry, and poetry in painting"—transcends structural tactics to embody a spatial rhythm guided by intuition, breaking conventions and reshaping patterns to evoke both surprise and emotional resonance. These poetic ruptures invite greater awareness and engagement with the space. Similarly, "Relaxed and Unrestrained Atmosphere" seeks to move beyond rigid spatial compositions by embracing a relaxed yet cohesive posture, allowing space to breathe with lightness and flexibility. Like brushwork in calligraphy or ink painting—marked by variations in brush pressure, ink's tonal contrast (*nōtan*), and intended blankness—this relaxed and unrestrained atmosphere establishes a natural rhythm between simplicity and richness, creating a dynamic contrast between openness and enclosure within the space.

In daily practice, I draw on both phenomenology and Eastern philosophy to reconsider the relationship between humans, space, and the cosmos. Space is not merely a physical container for activity; it is a way of being, resonating with philosopher Martin Heidegger's concept of "dwelling" and aligning with the Taoist worldview of harmony with nature. It unfolds as an ever-evolving realm—a temporal field, rather than a static geometry. Activated through movement, it embodies a spirit of wandering and holds a sensory rhythm that lets time flow through it. Drawing from philosopher Maurice Merleau-Ponty's theory of embodied perception, spatial experience is inextricably tied to body scale, sightlines, and movement. In a state of serenity, both mind and body resonate in harmony, and the spiritual essence of space lies in its responsiveness to the site and cultural context, much like the borrowed views (借景) and framed vistas (透景) in Chinese gardens. In this way, design becomes a medium for cultural continuity and the expression of regional identity.

At the same time, spatial design is also an art of *qi* cultivation, shaped by rhythm, restraint, and emptiness, fostering a subtle yet tangible atmosphere. This recalls Peter Zumthor's idea of architectural atmospheres—spaces that deeply move us but defy easy description. Within the urban context, I provide a gentle and thoughtful response to contemporary spiritual challenges, creating heterotopias within the city: spaces of otherness where the soul can rest. This approach allows for a mode of "reclusive dwelling without retreating from the world."

At the heart of my philosophy lies a design language, transcending visual style to be a perceptual structure and aesthetic system that surpasses time and place. It intertwines Eastern concepts such as *qi*, *yi*, void-form dynamics, and intentional blankness with modern rational design. By navigating thresholds and transitions, this language crafts a spatial expression that is both profound and unbounded, precise yet fluid. It responds not only to the formal demands of modern design but also to deeper human desires—for belonging, poetry, and spiritual anchoring. Straddling the line between form and spirit, the local and the global, I present a methodology rich in intellectual depth and emotional resonance—one that brings me back to the essence of design: making space a vessel of culture, a keeper of memory, and a sanctuary for the soul.

Contents

Tranquility

In the modern world, tranquility has become a luxury. It is not merely the quiet of physical space but a deep sense of inner peace. When the fast-paced life leaves one feeling "unmoored" (*unheimlichkeit*), and utilitarianism erodes individual will, tranquility emerges as a composite experience of the senses, emotions, and spirit. Through thoughtful design, people rediscover inner calm, turning a dwelling into a true "home." In modern Eastern spaces, tranquility manifests as a silent yet enduring presence, subtly infiltrating the smallest details of daily life. It operates as an invisible force, transforming a space into a vessel for emotions and thoughts, guiding individuals from the external clamor toward a sense of rootedness. With natural materials, meticulous details, and harmonious proportions, design not only expresses the quiet of the space but also fosters an atmosphere that invites self-reflection. Such tranquility evokes different images across cultures: the simple elegance of a Japanese tearoom, the embrace of landscape in a Chinese garden, and the rustic charm of stone cottages in the English countryside—all symbolizing an ideal serenity. It is a resonance of inner order, as though leaving a subtle distance between oneself and the world, and finding certainty within calm.

In the East, tranquility resembles the "cessation" (止息) found in Zen and Taoist practices. By slowing the rhythm of breath, one enters a state of relaxation and stillness, banishing inner turmoil and distraction. Sometimes, the spaces of tearooms and gardens, with their contemplative ambience, form the core of the experience—structures that seem to merge and separate, with soft lighting, natural materials, and a sense of spatial detachment, all working together to create a profound experience of tranquility. This tranquility transcends the external silence, achieved instead through inner dialogue and connection with oneself. At other times, tranquility takes the form of an ethereal "emptiness" experience, where movement and stillness blend. It is not the grandeur of marble echoing the midday sun, but rather the deep green shadows cast by tree branches through paper windows, swaying on the hanging paintings within. Landscape paintings and classical gardens use the technique of "leaving blank spaces" to create an open, fluid sense of a journey. When one gazes upon a painting, it feels as though one is stepping into it; in the garden, "changing vistas with every step" intertwine time and space, leading to moments of enlightenment. This type of tranquility channels more than just calm; it conveys the vitality of "time" and "space" through visual, mental, and spiritual shifts, reminiscent of the Taoist concept of "in extreme stillness, movement arises" (静极思动), or Peter Zumthor's idea that experiencing a space is "between composure and seduction."

The Chinese characters 谧 (*mì*, "serene") and 秘 (*mì*, "secret") not only share the same pronunciation but also reflect each other in their aesthetic sensibilities. *Jìngmì* (静谧), or tranquility, conveys a sense of simplicity and restraint, while *yǐnmì* (隐秘) or *yōumì* (幽秘) suggests secrecy, concealment, or an unfathomable depth of emotion. Both evoke a quietude untouched by intrusion, allowing one to sense a profound atmosphere in silence. Beneath the deep eaves of ancient Chinese wooden architecture, murals adorned with gold leaf or lacquerware inlaid with mother-of-pearl often remain shrouded in shadow, as if withholding their splendor. Only in the dim glow do they reveal a subdued shimmer—an interplay of light and darkness that renders opulence not as an overt display but as a perception, one that gently permeates the viewer's vision, evoking a quiet emergence of wonder and imagination.

As philosopher Walter Benjamin observed, true works of art possess an aura—a unique presence that sustains a tension between distance and intimacy, making the remote seem uncannily near. This quality resists mechanical reproduction and is deeply tied to the specific temporality and space of the viewing experience. The way space and light are orchestrated in Eastern Buddhist temples resonates with this concept. Deep eaves cast gradations of light and shadow, softening the brilliance of gold leaf and the vivid hues of cinnabar, lapis lazuli, and malachite that adorn sacred statues. Within the interwoven chiaroscuro, their radiance transforms into a quiet luminosity—one that softens the austerity of their presence, infusing solemnity with serenity, grandeur with restraint. Here, divinity does not reveal itself in stark clarity but in an aura of veiled luminescence. Light, filtering through high windows, diffusing from skylights, or glimmering against wooden beams, shapes an atmosphere that is impossible to replicate. The visage of the Buddha emerges gradually from the shifting shadows, as if suspended within an enigmatic realm. This experience—where the whole is never fully visible at once—compels the viewer to engage in a gradual unveiling, sensing tranquility and mystery through each nuanced transition of light and darkness. Every gaze uncovers a new detail, leaving behind an infinite space for contemplation.

This kind of expression, eloquent without explicit articulation, draws the viewer into the realm of the work without the need for direct persuasion. Rather than commanding attention, it exerts a quiet, imperceptible influence on the observer's state of mind, guiding them toward meditation and introspection. Even the most opulent colors, when veiled in shadow, attain composure—an intentional restraint that serves to move the soul. This synthesis of space, light, and materiality shapes an aura that is not only an aesthetic concealment but also a sanctity distilled through time. In that moment of quiet contemplation, the viewer experiences a solemn reverence—an ineffable transcendence. It is like the glow that surrounds the Buddha in a hushed temple hall, where every hue, texture, and craft reveals itself yet remains gently cradled within the stillness.

Given the multifaceted interpretations of tranquility, my design philosophy seeks delicate integration and soulful regeneration. In such a design language, materials are imbued with a sense of spontaneity, where each bamboo strip, each piece of wood, seemingly whispers its origin and potential. Proportions and colors are thoughtfully refined to present a natural, pure atmosphere, showcasing the beauty of "spiritual geometry." More importantly, through open layouts, simple lines, and fluid circulation, the design imbues stillness with a sense of movement, creating subtle tension between the interior and the exterior. But spaces that are too small or too grand can dilute the inherent mystery. An ideal tranquil space requires not only harmonious proportions and details but also consideration of human scale, finding balance between inclusion and freedom. Through such design, spaces achieve harmony between movement and stillness, as well as complexity and simplicity, ultimately resonating deeply with inner peace. The tranquility of the East is not forceful or contrived. Like water flowing freely, like flowers blooming on their own, it is not confined to external silence, allowing for the "occurrences" that arise naturally. This tranquility is inseparable from the subtle and delightful sounds that accompany it, just as the ancient Chinese said: "Stones make one ancient; water makes one distant. A garden's stones and water must never be absent." (石令人古, 水令人远。园林水石, 最不可无。) The silence of the stone may be profound, yet it is the subtle sounds of the garden that awaken it with quiet power, linking past and present, and evoking a tranquility beyond individual existence.

In the gardens of Suzhou, springs well up among the rocks, while rainwater slides off ancient tree branches, tapping against tiles and stone paths with crisp, delicate sounds. These small yet enchanting sounds anchor the soul and were cherished by ancient garden designers. Architecture becomes a finely tuned instrument, playing a unique melody with regional and cultural resonance. In a tranquil space, the sounds flow, allowing one to find balance and harmony between the material and the spiritual. Design begins and ends with poetry. We close the door and listen to the sound of water boiling; we open the door and hear the whisper of wind sweeping across the leaves. Tranquility is like the sound of a shakuhachi flute—at first, it is only a murmur, but it is only through penetrating the bamboo forest that its Zen-like meaning emerges in silence. Through these ordinary and quietly immersive experiences, spatial design allows the material world to reveal its spiritual power, presenting a profound existence interwoven with sensory and intellectual depth.

Air

空氣

Though formless, air holds the most delicate and enduring trace of space. The skin feels the breeze. The nose catches a scent. Geometry recedes. Then light stirs the sea, as briny air renders the harbor dreamlike. Paper and wood hint at forests and hidden streams. In the unseen, space breathes while time slips quietly into the seams of body and soul.

What do we mean when we talk about the quality of space? In the past, before existentialism and phenomenology, the answer might have been: proportion, scale, structure, and volume—spatial attributes like these. Today, however, we realize that invisible elements also shape a space—namely, its atmosphere and microclimate. For a home that captures a true sense of comfort, its space quality stems from a subtle exchange: a continuous dialogue between the house and its environment. Stepping into such a space brings to mind words like "flow" and "tactility." This is made possible by air—through breezes, scents, and even the atmospheric character of space—an essential yet often overlooked component of design. Whether it's the gentle wind through a courtyard or a faint fragrance lingering in the air, these elements harmonize through design into a deeply perceptible experience.

Design isn't merely about shaping the tangible; it's about guiding the senses and emotions. The largest organ of the human body is the skin, making touch our first point of contact with space. Air, in motion, gathers sound and fragrance, subtly influencing a space's cultural attributes. This perception goes beyond direct experience, stirring memories that dwell beneath awareness. For instance, in *The Book of Tea*, Okakura Tenshin describes a poetic, multisensory scene: the sound of a boiling iron kettle resembles that of misty waterfalls, waves crashing against rocks, or wind rustling through bamboo. These sounds and sensations form a multidimensional landscape. Similarly, a small town along the Mediterranean coast offers a different sensory polyphony. Sunlight cascades onto golden beaches, while the scent of ripe fruit merges with sea salt in the air—and all of it becomes memory. Air, through temperature, humidity, movement, and scent, delivers an ineffable experience, shaping the space we feel before we even see it.

In spatial design, water serves as the ideal medium for air. In the Sanya Haitang Bay project, the humidity of the sea breeze, the fragrance of plants, and the interaction of airflow combine to give the space rich, dynamic qualities. By incorporating water, wind temperature is moderated, offering a cool, comfortable tactile experience. More importantly, the fusion of water and air reshapes the sensory experience: it's neither just the sea breeze nor the fresh scent of the garden, but a novel and unique "flavor" of space. Through light curtains and hemp installations, designers make the flow of air visible. As the wind moves these materials, the resulting visual tremors dissolve spatial inertia, mingling with light and shadow to create a soft, fluid sense of place. The moisture and scents awaken memories, imbuing the space with a strong sense of locality and cultural belonging. The design of air permeates multiple sensory dimensions—smell, touch, and vision—culminating in an experience of situational thinking. This reminds us that humans are in a continuous dialogue with space.

In Eastern philosophy, air (or *qi*) symbolizes freedom, flow, and the impermanence of life. Through architecture, air conveys a sense of connection and unity, like water brushing against skin, blurring the boundaries between self and world. The warmth, coolness, moisture, or dryness of air influences our interpretation of space, turning its creation and experience into a slow, profound drift. If the architectural history of the past centuries reflects the oscillation between reason and emotion, between subjective and objective perspectives, then today, by designing with the invisible element of air, we connect the material and the conscious. In doing so, architecture opens a deeper dimension—between reality and dream, image and memory.

Sanya Haitang Bay

Sanya, China – December 2023

Contract Room

Page 22 The longing for sojourn is a call to future memories. The Sanya Haitang Bay project offers an unconventional coastal retreat, where space flows, boundaries dissolve. Light, water, and air gently mingle. Rather than portraying the sea, the design evokes it through sensation, awakening harmony between body and nature. In this quiet interplay, purity meets belonging, and the sea within, though silent, pulses with inner strength.

Pages 24–25 The subtropical climate brings a moist sea breeze, with filtered sunlight casting soft shadows through dense foliage. In the nearly 5-meter-high (16-foot-high) reception hall, organic ultra-high performance concrete (UHPC) walls emphasize natural textures, while the water feature and bamboo lattices enhance airflow, fostering a calm, shaded serenity.

Pages 26–27 The bamboo lattice pavilion creates a serene, airy space, where black wooden floors and limestone tables form a rhythmic contrast, infusing vitality into the calm.

Pages 28–29 In the ground-floor indoor courtyard, the water flows seamlessly, filling the space with a lingering moisture in the air.

Pages 30–31 Without superfluous decoration, the space cultivates a serene, restrained atmosphere through contrasting textures, diffused light, and sculpted rhythms. Bamboo lattices separate yet connect, letting breeze and light weave a layered sensory experience. The white staircase's monolithic handrail recalls modernist purity, guiding deeper contemplation. The end wall, articulated in a painterly logic of proportion and material, brings a composed sense of ritual to the space.

Pages 32–33 In key circulation areas, warm and bright bamboo pavilions guide the gaze.

Pages 34–35 The bamboo pavilion at the parking entrance, framed in black, mirrors the main entrance, ensuring a cohesive and inviting atmosphere.

Opposite page The seaside café is a fusion of modern spirit and tropical charm. Soft curtains gently divide the space, adjusting the light from the skylight above. The design goes beyond the visible, creating a sensory experience.

This page The white sofa area invites relaxation, as the sea breeze blends with the gentle air from the indoor water garden.

The sea breeze softly stirs the linen drapes, creating a delicate rhythm that transforms the café into a garden within a garden.

As an interventional element, the sculpture, with its coarse textures, responds to the space's restrained vocabulary. It forms a dynamic tension between the linen drape and the latticework, guiding the visual path and initiating a dialogue between materials. Light and shadow animate its contours, intertwining with its structural lines, allowing the art to become part of the spatial constitution itself.

Previous spread The bamboo lattice pavilion forms a private VIP lounge, with a large shelving unit and linen curtains that enhance its peacefulness and privacy. The unadorned petrified wood stumps support the tea table, echoing the wood carvings in the corner and fostering a relaxed ambiance. A soft, cozy, cross-patterned rug enriches the tactile experience while subtly defining the space, bringing harmony and order to the overall layout.

This page The private dining space is anchored in deep brown and warm gold. Bamboo lattice panels introduce rhythm and transparency, delineating spaces with a permeable division that flows rather than obstructs. A cloudlike gilded pendant light reinforces the vertical axis. At the center, a round table reflects the communal, intimate spirit of Eastern dining. Light is purposefully restrained—focused on the tabletop, while the periphery recedes into shadow—fostering quiet intimacy and understated elegance.

Opposite page A large golden installation serves as the perceptual focal point of the space. Its abstract form and gold-leaf-like texture capture the essence of light, as if holding a suspended moment of sunset. As sunlight glides over its surface, the material seems quietly awakened, revealing subtle changes that make the piece a mediator among time, light, and spatial perception.

Enigma

探幽

To seek the hidden depths is to enter a spatial play, where, like a quiet summer treat, a cool and soothing calm is slowly savored amid deep, serene, and hazy light, evoking the leisurely sentiment of the East.

Those who have delved into the nuances of ancient Asian ways of life often observe that, rather than embracing the straightforward, East Asian cultures gravitate toward a delicate dance of subtlety and veiled emotions. For instance, in traditional East Asian interiors, paper windows stand in stark contrast to the modern glass panes, which lay bare every corner of the world outside and within. These delicate windows are also unlike the solid stone walls of ancient castles, which sever all connection with the exterior. Instead, they echo the delicate *xuan* paper of landscape paintings, permitting light to filter softly through. As the glow within fades across the room, memories seem to drift away. Similarly, East Asian cuisine and artifacts emanate a quiet, understated beauty: lacquered vessels adorned with gold leaf or mother-of-pearl, whether as dinnerware, a screen, or a cabinet tucked away in a corner, exude an elegance that flourishes in the shadows; the morsels, cool and refreshing at first glance, invite a serene and reflective mood, as though each bite whispers a moment of calm introspection.

It is in this dim, muted light that one's thoughts settle, awakening a gentle sense of leisure and tranquility. Excessive brightness brings quick satisfaction and clear goals, whereas the "subtle" atmosphere evokes a desire for careful appreciation, prompting emotions and pleasures beyond function and reason. East Asians have long avoided the direct, embracing instead the interplay between "hidden" and "apparent," "open" and "secret," much like the "virtual and real" dynamics in paintings. It is in these elusive moments that the joy of seeking mystery and beauty is found. Thus, *tan-you* (探幽), literally "exploring the depths of the hidden" or "seeking the quiet mystery," can be viewed as a kind of rhythm that unveils the subtle relationship between space and action. It is a slow unfolding of depth, intrigue, and wonder—akin to a garden stroll, where secrets reveal themselves step by step. This is not merely a visual experience but an embodied dialogue between the self and space. With each corner turned and every pause taken, the space comes alive and starts to breathe. In light that ebbs and flows, the journey feels like walking through a mist-veiled forest toward a hidden temple, a storied rock, or a lone pine, inviting a sensory pilgrimage that extends beyond sight. In Eastern gardens, this experience becomes a "never-ending flow" of space. Through ingenious layouts and the choreography of nature, the visitor is gently guided into a realm of shifting shadows and layered depths. Here, movement becomes meditation—each step stirring a quiet urge to explore, to contemplate, and to rediscover the fleeting grace of things.

In traditional architectural design, one is rarely granted a direct line of sight from the entrance through the corridors, gardens, or inner structures beyond. Ancient garden designers employed multiple visible and hidden openings, transitional spaces between rooms, and undulating corridors to evoke a sense of infinite unfolding. For example, halls are often laid out in three and a half or four and a half spatial units, with the "half unit" being the key to evoking surprise or mystery. Corridors, shaped by the natural topography, curve and meander, sometimes climbing the hillside or spanning over water, full of variation, as though one were entering a secluded valley. The pleasure of *tan-you*—of exploring the subtle and secret—lies in drifting through space and time in a gentle haze, where accidental encounters and quiet revelations awaken the senses. Walls are not fully enclosed, but leave openings and apertures through which light and scenery softly filter in. Pavilions and other garden structures often incorporate elements like bead curtains or wooden screens inside, softly filtering views into fragmented glimpses—a delicate balance of the real and the imagined. Corridors are designed to appear segmented, creating an illusion of dead ends, only to disclose new scenes at each turn, and staircases often avoid the central axis, merging into the terrain, deepening the atmosphere of concealment and discovery.

A modern interpretation of such spatial design can be found in The Fame project. Its layout follows the garden principle of "not revealing everything at once," weaving together direct light, gentle reflection on floor tiles, and the soft refraction and diffusion through art glass to conjure a dreamlike atmosphere. Light filters through pressed bamboo strips, softening the boundary between real and surreal, bathing the space in an ethereal glow. A suspended installation, *Fish Becoming a Dragon* emits light in response to the water flanking the hall's pathways, appearing as a spiritual symbol drawn from dreams. Meanwhile, concrete walls with cascading eave-like structures, infused with quartz sand, bear the texture of erosion, inviting touch, as though one were stepping into the timeworn hush of an ancient garden, where the tactile meets the poetic. Similarly, the Central Manor project invites a comparable journey of exploration. Peacock-green ceramic tiles allude to ancient porcelain craftsmanship of the East, blending the salon seamlessly into the surrounding lush cedar forest. Inside, stone steps intentionally avoid a direct entrance path, guiding visitors around large green square columns, whose articulated surfaces recall the segmented form of bamboo, before ascending gracefully to the upper floor. Along the way, vertical wall sconces cast a soft white glow onto sedimentary rock walls in muted gray—like spring water trickling over stones. As Ming dynasty scholar Ye Xie once said, such a space embodies the aesthetic spirit of "faint and ethereal as reason, imagined as matter, fleeting and vague as emotion (幽渺以为理, 想象以为事, 惝恍以为情)." Here, space becomes poetry—a retreat from function into an atmosphere of elegance and subtle revelation.

The Fame

Chengdu, China – April 2024

Page 48 Light, filtered through frosted glass, lends a hushed clarity, while bamboo lattice softens the edges of form and enclosure. At the turning point, the two materials orchestrate a rhythmic passage—parted yet connected—guiding the wanderer through a quiet choreography of unfolding views. The glow strips away superficiality; *you*—the hidden—is not merely a visual haze but a descent into the psyche. *Tan* (exploration) becomes an inward journey, a quiet return to the self.

Opposite page As Ming literati once said, "Living amid mountains and waters is ideal, followed by village life, with suburban living as the next best." In the heart of the city, a salonlike gathering space becomes a peaceful sanctuary, nestled within lush greenery, offering an inviting escape.

This page Viewed from the courtyard, a Zen chair—balancing modern sensibilities with ancient charm—embodies the dialogue between body and environment. The interior and exterior unfold into one another, softening the threshold between them.

Following spread In the grand and serene hall, low-slung furniture is paired with black finishes that recall the texture of rain-washed mountain rocks. A quiet spirit of unadorned antiquity lingers within this contemporary space. Here, beside the pines, people gather in soft conversation, immersed in a shared sense of ease and connection.

This page The intentionally sloped walls evoke the quiet thrill of peering and discovery, reminiscent of Eastern garden strolls, where glimpses of rockeries emerge unexpectedly along the way.

Opposite page Upon closer inspection, the black finishes, with their cascading "eave" structures, recall the quiet mountain chalets after rain, infusing the space with intimacy and subtle tension. The enigmatic wall lamp quietly guides one's movement.

A potted pine captures the untamed beauty of Chengdu's mountains and forests, bringing a touch of nature's wild allure indoors.

The velvety softness of the armchairs contrasts beautifully with the sturdy presence of the low wooden table. Light and shadow filtered through the lattices further unify the two, infusing the space with a quiet, lived-in charm.

The light gray stone underfoot evokes the ambiance of mountain forests. With a form that bridges bed and seat, the platform sofa offers both rest and display, akin to the open-air *tà* (榻 , reclining couch) in ancient paintings, capturing the leisure of seclusion in nature.

This page The light-colored marble creates an elevated entrance, with steps leading up, forming a bodily transition from the hall to the interior corridor.

Following pages The dining space, enveloped in pristine limestone, contrasts with the atmosphere of the previous space, creating a dramatic spatial rhythm between tranquility and expansiveness.

Previous spread Stepping into the art hall surrounded by bamboo strips, the renowned local bamboo sea is seamlessly integrated into modern design. The interplay of bamboo, bronze, and marble reflects the spirit of the place, fermenting the essence of "slow" living.

Opposite page The narrative qualities of Eastern spaces are carved into the hall through the *Fish Becoming a Dragon* shadow puppet installation, demonstrating my commitment to "total design."

This page This ancient motif of prosperity is carved into three dimensions from local translucent leather. Suspended amid flowing water flanking the walkway and a mirrored ceiling, it becomes a luminous presence, like moonlight under the sea, pulling the viewer into a quiet reverie where self dissolves and memories float away, elusive and fleeting.

Following spread As the water vanishes, a bridge spans across; the water feature beside the marble path ebbs and flows, creating a rhythmic interplay of space. The walls on either side, crafted from contrasting materials, initiate a conversation between past and present, guiding one toward a serene dwelling.

Central Manor

Chongqing, China – April 2022

Page 68 The reception foyer forms a quiet countercurrent to urban noise—a gradual, calming transition rather than a direct entry. Light guides the path; stone columns, under wall-washing lights, recall ancient steles. Volcanic stone flooring absorbs glare, drawing the eye inward, while a metal-toned wooden lattice ceiling lowers the visual center, heightening the space's sense of depth and seclusion.

Previous spread A residence built in a mountain city should evoke a sense of retreat. The volcanic-stone foyer wraps the body in cool stillness. Beyond, the hall opens wide. At its far end, floor-to-ceiling glass frames a view of the distant valley, where rising mist whispers the residence's lakeside setting. As one walks inward, elongated wall sconces, aligned in vertical rhythm, emit a soft, pearly glow against dark gray stone—like hidden springs glistening beneath forest stones.

Opposite page The outdoor water feature extends into the interior, separated yet continuous, leading toward a jade pavilion outlined in washed brass, exuding an airy sense of solemnity.

This page The body's movement aligns with the evolving spatial functions. Like admiring the rock formations in an Eastern garden, the path begins at the side and gradually leads to the front, revealing the distinct character of each scene.

Previous spread By carefully selecting and proportioning materials, a space can achieve a layered yet unified feel. The key is balancing the visual weight of materials to create harmony.

This page The peacock-green ceramic panels bring a touch of woodland charm to the space, while the brass and white jade staircase railing adds a sense of fluidity to the staircase structure. "Enigma" embodies the rhythmic interplay of stillness and motion, evoking the essence of mountain and water landscapes.

A sofa upholstered in verdant green velvet, paired with a gray-green marble inset side table, adds a tactile weight to the peaceful feel. The realm of *tan-you* translates design into a spiritual illumination.

Transitioning from deep shadows to light, the expansive skylight defines the tea room's boundary, making walls unnecessary. The large lacquered tea table enhances the sense of scale, anchoring the flow of the space.

Garden

The garden of the East does not abide by the measures of time. Ancient yet immediate, it draws forth the quiet power of space, calling the mind inward. Between absence and presence, the finite holds the infinite, guiding the body and spirit to wander and dwell.

In Eastern culture, classical gardens play a vital role in both everyday life and spiritual contemplation. When nature is integrated into human living spaces, gardens naturally take form, as quiet thresholds between the inner self and the outer world. From the open courtyard of a teahouse to the grand architectural poetry of Beijing's Old Summer Palace and the refined elegance of Kyoto's Katsura Imperial Villa, each becomes a unique embodiment of this timeless philosophy and enduring tradition. Beyond mere dwellings, Eastern gardens serve as extensions of the soul and microcosms of nature. As architect Walter Gropius once noted, while Western thought often turns outward to master the material world, Eastern philosophy seeks breakthroughs within the inner realm. Gardens, in essence, embody this wisdom.

At the heart of integrating ancient garden artistry into contemporary spatial design lies the creation of an immersive, exploratory experience. Whether it is a single stone or an entire garden, every element should invite wandering and contemplation. Consider the rockeries in Suzhou's Lingering Garden: Taihu stones are artfully stacked to evoke distant peaks or arranged to mimic undulating ridgelines. As one meanders around them, shifting perspectives unfold like a handscroll—each step revealing a new composition, subtle in detail yet infinite in interpretation. This transformation—from static form to dynamic experience—encapsulates the poetic spirit of Eastern gardens. Even a solitary scholar's rock, with its "perforation (漏), pervasion (透), lank (瘦), and rugosity (皱)" characteristics, offers an ever-shifting interplay of light and shadow, presence and void, allowing the observer to uncover myriad layers of meaning. Beyond rock gardens, elements such as moon gates, pierced windows, and meandering water features along the winding corridors are choreographed to orchestrate sightlines, modulate rhythm, and enrich perception. A garden is never meant to be grasped in a single glance but to be wandered, discovered, and quietly inhabited. As the Chinese garden designers wisely said, "A garden may take form even in the absence of trees and woods."

To sustain the essence of this philosophy in modern design, it is vital to uphold the seamless interrelationship between human, architecture, and environment. The goal is not replication but transposition—translating the spirit of "changing vistas at every step" into contemporary spatial vocabulary, evoking a multisensory resonance. I achieve this by reinterpreting the spatial logic of classical gardens: the winding corridors, layered thresholds, and modulated flows are recast as atria, entrances, and transitional spaces. Vertical and horizontal apertures open onto walls, guiding sightlines and drawing in natural light, air, and landscape, turning interiors into galleries of shifting atmosphere. Here, the architecture becomes both shelter and scenery: one is enclosed by walls yet brushed by mountain breeze, touched by dappled light and immersed in landscape. Even absent of flora, the space breathes through light, texture, and rhythm, echoing the garden's gentle dialectic between nature and the built.

It is through this contemporary design language that the spatial sensibility of classical gardens can be meaningfully translated across new typologies. In the Urban Garden project, for instance, the garden experience unfolds underground. A sculptural staircase, inspired by the twisting gesture of mountains, becomes a vertical anchor—its form mirrored by hexagonal basalt formations in the water feature below. When the soft wind glides over the water, the dialogue between light, stone, and human movement dissolves the density of the subterranean setting, restoring a sense of breath and openness.

Likewise, in the Riverside Mansion project, the concept of a garden is elevated into vertical living. A contemplative moss-and-fern arrangement in the living room evokes the scholar's rock in miniature. The subtly raised corridor, linking the study and reception room, reintroduces the cadence of garden wanderings, where one steps up and then meanders down in a rhythmic flow. This poetic design transforms the apartment into an "elevated garden in the sky," a quiet intervention that transcends the stark rationality of modernist structures and infuses contemporary living with warmth and humanistic spirit. In an era increasingly dominated by industrialization and speed, the importance of gardens becomes ever more pronounced. Designing a garden is more than landscaping; it is the creation of a profound spatial experience—one that preserves and extends the sensory and emotional richness of classical garden strolls. In a way, the garden is not just seen but felt. It is through the choreography of stillness and motion, in the quiet succession of vistas, that one rediscovers a deeper rhythm of life, measured not by urgency but by presence.

Riverside Mansion

Hangzhou, China – June 2022

Page 84 Amid the urban jungle of concrete and steel, nature is a rarity. Rooted in Eastern traditions, this design responds to nature by shaping interior topographies. Gently rising platforms, embedded courtyards, and potted landscapes form a walkable, livable path. Greenery echoes distant mountains beyond the window, creating a layered "interior *shanshui*." Materials, textures, and plantings guide the gaze softly, like shifting views in a classical garden.

Opposite page The fireplace serves as the space's spiritual focal point. The three-material wall blends warmth and coolness, transforming the modern fireplace into a scene of ancient people warming themselves in the mountains. The stone sculpture above combines ancient aura with modern protection, merging time and space into a unique charm.

Previous spread From the foyer, the living room with floor-to-ceiling windows frames views of the mountains and skyline. A low table with brass-etched textures mimics wood, while an embedded moss garden brings nature indoors, balancing rationality with natural ambiance.

Opposite page Viewed from the living room, the tea room's wall, composed of light stone tiles and aged brass, offers a modern interpretation of ancient Eastern screens. It leaves a gap at the bottom, through which one can glimpse a low tea table and its elegant white porcelain teaware.

Following spread The tearoom and living room face each other, separated yet connected by the screen wall. While sipping tea and conversing, one can glimpse the moss and ferns in the living room. To see partially is to let concealment reveal.

Opposite page "To create the illusion of endless water, a bridge should span its break," said the Ming dynasty garden designer Ji Cheng. The marble stepping stones cleverly conceal the water's end, creating an illusion of infinite space. The downward-facing wall light, shaped like a black stone, is discreetly placed at the base, while plant shadows on the wall blend with the mountain view outside, resembling an ink painting.

Following spread The study unfolds along the corridor, adorned on the left wall with irregular ceramic artworks, a desk and chairs midway, and the distant skyline framed beyond. Echoing the shifting views of a scholar's garden, the spatial rhythm draws the body forward toward a soft glow at the corridor's end. Wall ceramics and curated objects evoke moss-covered rocks, composing a micro-landscape of quiet resonance.

This page Linen blinds soften the harsh light, bathing the room in a gentle glow. As one gazes into the distance, the skyline and mountain contours gradually emerge.

Opposite page The woven rattan tea mat exudes subtle scents of grass and bark, reminiscent of freshly cut bamboo and dried grain stalks.

Following spread The tearoom and study are connected by half-height antique brass screens, subtly oxidized to resemble weathered wood. The corridor linking the living room, tearoom, and study, with varying elevations, evokes the sensation of strolling through a garden.

Urban Garden

Hangzhou, China – May 2024

Page 102 Eastern gardens have long navigated between two rhythms: the geometric clarity of distilled nature and spirit, and the relaxed pace of a continuous, contemplative journey. In the reception hall, light permeates horizontally and vertically, falling upon undulating volumes and moss, diffusing between materials and air. This creates a quiet, restrained, and profound atmosphere that gently leads visitors into a transcendent state of mind.

Opposite page At the hall entrance, light cascades, casting shadows that merge with the wooden structure, adding depth.

This page A breeze flows between enclosed and open spaces, connecting the interior garden with the outdoor water feature. The scholars' rock in the corner guides one into the black-box transition room, leading to a more private social area.

The fireplace wall, like a black lacquered screen, divides the lounge into two distinct yet connected areas. The ledge above the fireplace holds flowers, plants, and antiques.

This page As the heart of the lounge, the central bar beneath the overhanging eaves resembles an Eastern pavilion, evoking a deep cultural familiarity that brings a sense of comfort and tranquility.

Following spread Beside the openwork fireplace, the glow enhances wine tasting and conversation. Through the fireplace, one can meet a friend's gaze while enjoying the courtyard view, deepening the moment with serenity and connection.

Looking up from the water garden on the basement level, the artistic staircase becomes the visual focal point, vertically extending the space and infusing it with dynamic energy.

This page The extensive use of travertine creates a cavelike ambiance, with light and shadow shifting to reveal the powerful forces of nature.

Following spread As light and shadow fade, a serene atmosphere envelops the space. The re-cut stone sculptures on the water surface, arranged like scattered stones in an Eastern garden, radiate a natural energy that connects with the surroundings. As one moves, the artistic staircase and water reflect on the mirrored walls, creating a dreamlike effect.

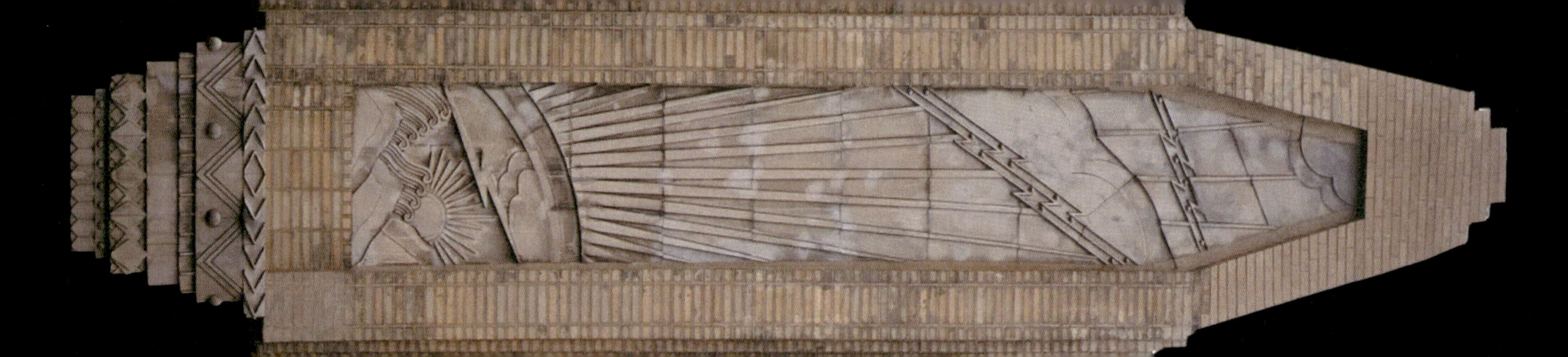

Nostalgia

懷舊

Nostalgia is a creative emotion, a postponed return to one's homeland. It requires not only relics of the past but also the power of imaginative insight to unravel confusion.

Getting acquainted with a city begins with nostalgia for its past. It starts with a few well-remembered scents, unfolds into a scene of déjà vu, and gradually fades into thoughts of the future—much like Marcel Proust's portrayal of the tea-soaked madeleine in *In Search of Lost Time* or Gustave Caillebotte's delicate sketch of rain-dampened street, evoking a profound longing for Paris. Today, people yearn to touch the traces of the past, whether it's London's iconic red phone booths, the Vienna Café Chair, or Lisbon's signature yellow Tram 28. Yet nostalgia demands more than mere artifacts of a bygone era, which would otherwise render the present an empty museum. True nostalgia carries vitality; it does not linger in a simplistic return to the past but encourages us forward, reinterpreting and reconstructing memories.

When recalling Shanghai's golden age, one cannot overlook its vibrant social life. People strolled along the rivers, played violins, and watched the sun set. It is often said, not without a sense of humor and affection, that every great city rises by a great river: Paris has the Seine, London the Thames, New York the Hudson, and Shanghai the Huangpu River and Suzhou Creek. These rivers, the cradle of urban civilization, not only bear the weight of a city's history and memory but also embody a dynamic and open spirit.

Meanwhile, the skyscrapers lining the riverbanks stand as bold testaments to modern ambition and urban power. Take, for instance, the Shanghai Mansion (formerly the Broadway Mansions), poised at the confluence of the Suzhou and Huangpu Rivers. This architectural landmark was a spiritual beacon of its time, blending art deco elegance with American modernism. Its façade, clad at the base in richly veined, highly polished dark green marble, exudes a quiet grandeur. One can almost imagine swaying gently to jazz on the terraces, gazing upon the riverside—a tableau of Shanghai's bustling glamour a century ago. As new buildings rise along the Suzhou Creek, we seek to reconstruct memories of the past within contemporary spaces—such as in Domus. Nostalgia, after all, is the art of repeating the unrepeatable, of giving form to the immaterial. At the heart of the salon, a water feature becomes the centerpiece for gatherings, where people sip and chat, perhaps even waltz. The pool becomes a symbol of time's passage, fostering a silent dialogue between architecture and the river, water and stone. Alabaster columns and a bar counter, walls clad in Amazon green marble and antique brass, accented by exquisite wall lights, guide us toward a stage where the past comes alive. In such a nostalgic mansion, splendor and melancholy intertwine, radiating a vibrant energy.

Nostalgia, therefore, is both retrospective and forward-looking. It draws on whimsical fantasies of a bygone era to dispel confusion and, while respecting history, creates spatial experiences that resonate in the present and hold promise for the future. Continuing Shanghai's elegance and fervor within living spaces becomes a vital endeavor. In designing Arbour, I envisioned residents as directors of their lives, with their space serving as an intimate theater. Every fragment of the city's past finds its echo: a balcony beneath golden plane trees, a living room overlooking red-brick houses, or a banquet hall screening vintage films. Wine-red marble and warm wood paneling render these memories tangible and vivid, weaving them into the fabric of daily life. As French philosopher Gaston Bachelard once wrote:

And the old house
I feel its russet warmth
Comes from the senses to the mind.

Descending from the second floor to the living room and onward to the screening room, the leisurely pace defies the linearity of modern time. We long to stretch and meander through time, much like returning to the innocent delights of childhood. In this sense, nostalgic spaces transcend archaeological explorations of a specific era or location, offering a universal solace. They transform history into personal or collective mythologies, inviting the residents to visit time as they visit space. As the interior unfolds, the scene before the eyes of those living in Arbour mirrors a gentle walk that once led from those shaded lanes to the Cathay Theatre in Shanghai. In the courtyard, a quiet fountain deepens the memory.

It must be understood that a modern individual's identity is forged at the intersection of tradition and the future. In adapting to globalization and digitalization, we need "objects of distinction" to differentiate the local from the universal. The true significance of nostalgia thus lies in its ability to offer a new understanding of time and space. Such a space does not merely honor the past, but it becomes a temporal utopia, where the relentless march of time is momentarily suspended. It is a place for contemplation, a garden that permits forgetting. Here, life is lived with the glow of bygone days. For design, nostalgia becomes a creative sentiment—a return to a home we have yet reached, granting us the freedom to narrate and reinvent the past.

Domus

Shanghai, China – November 2023

Page 118 The golden age's spirit arose from seeking order amid contradictions—a clash of reason and emotion, blending future hope with nostalgia. The salon hall's symmetrical layout, antique brass, green marble, and carefully crafted light and shadow evoke 1920s Shanghai's charm and prosperity. Eschewing excess decoration, the design uses structure, material contrast, and volume proportions to create a cinematic, dramatic space recalling classic Shanghai scenes.

Pages 120–121 The central pool at the salon hall denotes the slow passage of time, as materiality sets the rhythm of interconnected spaces, linking nostalgic, intricate scenes of quiet beauty.

Page 122 The antique brass and green marble finishes, bathed in sunlight, fill the space with the metropolitan aura of old Shanghai. Inspired by the Broadway Mansions, the brass sconces evoke a sense of the past.

Page 123 A few steps from the sofa lead to floor-to-ceiling windows, offering a stunning view of the Suzhou Creek through wooden shutters. The standing sculpture blends ancient presence with a vision of the future.

Pages 124–125 The large floral arrangement softens the space, harmonizing the textures. The natural wood of the sofa and the antique brass finishes on the walls reveal the marks of time.

Page 126 Four tall alabaster columns with integrated lighting in the salon's "traffic core" exude stability and strength, enhancing the space's verticality while blending natural patterns with artificial design for a striking effect.

Page 127 The three-tiered marble steps offer a gardenlike bodily experience as one ascends or descends, with the change in elevation amplifying the sensation.

Opposite page The "L"-shaped sofa features steps at both ends, cleverly creating a cyclical, promenade-like experience in the VIP room.

This page The recessed bar counter, elevated from the sofa area, enhances interaction and service. Its brass finish and geometric segmentation balance vintage and avant-garde, adding artistic tension. The sofa back separates the two floor heights in the VIP lounge. The elevation change fosters an intriguing spatial experience.

Previous spread The long sofa and minibar counter recall the refined bars of Shanghai's golden era. The golden velvet armchairs pair with a black patterned rug, blending elegance with grandeur. Teak walls soften the hard green marble and brass finishes, adding warmth and approachability to the space. The handcrafted tea brick table, made of square pieces resembling ink blocks, reveals a jade-like mosaic under sunlight, subtly evoking Eastern memories through its scent.

Opposite page A semi-independent exhibition space within the salon, accessible through the lobby and elevator hall, features a jade-green marble structure that exudes a calm, nostalgic vibe. White glass filters the light, creating a soft, dawnlike glow, perfect for showcasing artworks.

MIKE BIDLO / NOT MARSDEN HARTLEY
RED BOOK
READING CY TWOMBLY

Arbour

Shanghai, China – November 2024

Page 134 The "past" we cherish often reflects present emotions. Scenes, colors, sounds, and figures we recall glisten with an idealized glow through memory's lens. In the oak-enclosed living room, a white sofa awakens the old house's soul. By reimagining traditional spatial boundaries, the design crafts a contemporary order. Soft lighting, a spiral staircase's curves, and refined vintage furnishings compose a quiet, elegant "indoor theater," evoking a century-old French villa where time and nostalgia entwine.

This page Seen from the foyer, the dining table and chairs in the open kitchen feature a clever design: when tucked in, they transform into a geometric flower stand facing the courtyard; when pulled out, their actual function is revealed.

Opposite page The armchair, with its curved back inspired by Ming chairs, echoes the central coffee table of staggered geometric blocks. The handcrafted metal staircase enhances the space's openness, while the soft light and gentle steps echo the passage of time.

Following pages (left) In the basement banquet space, the white linen curtains draw open like a stage curtain. The off-center chandelier breaks symmetry, creating a more intimate dining atmosphere.

Following pages (right) The dining area and bar evoke both nostalgia and anticipation. The red marble dining table and velvet sofas recall the bricks of old houses, with rich, understated colors, much like the warm, mellow notes time imparts to wine.

SAKAMOTO

Previous spread The spaces for solitude and socializing are distinct. Upstairs, raw oak bookshelves create a cozy study, with a wool rug softening time and a distressed leather chair deepening it. A vintage speaker embedded in the bookshelf plays music, reviving the soul of old Shanghai.

This page The entire three floors are dedicated to private living. In the oak-clad bedroom, a thick wool rug and flickering fireplace create a cozy atmosphere, while softly draped curtains invite peaceful slumber. On restful mornings and afternoons, the bed bench offers a spot to rest or lean, allowing thoughts to drift.

Beneath the original attic, the closet and bathtub are nestled, while the fireplace adds a serene ambiance to this tall, light-filled space. The presence of the French plane trees feels almost dreamlike.

Placing the walk-in closet and bathtub by the balcony is a bold choice. To the soft melody, wrapped in a bathrobe and stepping onto the balcony recreates the century-old charm of Shanghai life. The carved iron railing, metal door handles, and dappled light through the plane trees all reflect the enduring influence of French living.

Memories

记忆

Memory's power lies in its fluidity. Spatial design softens the boundary between past and present, allowing memory to reshape itself through the continual weaving of time and gesture. Like a river that folds back on itself, drifting, settling, and flowing on, it quietly forms a field where time and space become perceptible.

Shanghai, nestled by both sea and river, was once a quintessential Jiangnan water town before its port opening in 1848. Amid their fishing, the fishermen would occasionally straighten their backs to behold the mesmerizing sight of reeds swaying in the breeze. These lush reed beds were not just nature's gift but also an essential part of daily life, woven into fish baskets, rustic ornaments, and even used to build huts, holding cherished childhood memories and embodying the serene, poetic essence of the water town. Centuries ago, Shanghai, a coastal town with little political significance, attracted scholars and disillusioned officials seeking refuge from the turmoil of the world. During the Jiajing period of the Ming dynasty (1522–1566), when the city walls were built, there were already twenty known gardens that graced its interior, including the still-preserved Yu Garden. It can be said that, long before its port opening, Shanghai had cultivated a unique local culture defined by nonconformity, entrepreneurial spirit, and inclusivity. Today, however, when people think of Shanghai, they often envision its modern persona as the "Magic City," and the memories of the old Jiangnan water town slowly fade into the past.

As the tidal flats along the Huangpu River gave way to grand international architecture, the once-present coastal reeds became increasingly hard to find. Not without a sense of loss, I designed the fine dining space Hai Shang near the Bund, aiming to offer a moment of serenity amid the bustling city. In the soft, diffused light, delicate reeds are stacked in circular formations, evoking the first dreamlike scene—one that seems to quietly await the arrival of time travelers. The bold sense of volume enhances the texture of the materials, crafting an almost surreal space. In the softly dimmed ambiance, the simple, natural textures and subtle scents awaken memories of the reed beds by the sea, creating a spatial experience that is familiar yet distant. Light grazes the slender black column near the entrance, revealing a quiet threshold into the space within. As visitors walk toward it, their gaze lingers on the simple hand-carved wooden plaque, where the restaurant's name is inscribed. Then, following the rough stone steps recalling childhood, they proceed through a narrow corridor flanked by weathered wooden walls, where the sound of flowing water softly washes away the noise of the city. One must first forget something in order to remember it. A sufficiently deep path carves out a silence—a blank space—allowing memory to emerge.

At the dining area, reclaimed beams from one of the historic districts remain exposed across the ceiling in their weathered state—a quiet tribute to material memory and a direct link to the past. This minimalist gesture isn't about flaunting rarity but about conveying a quiet strength veiled in the irretrievable passage of time. The brass chandelier, patinated over the years, bears the layered imprint of time. Concrete walls, etched with the grain of old wood, meet other charcoal-black wooden finishes, grounding the space in a calm, elemental palette. Humble and restrained, the atmosphere channels the cultivated spirit of Jiangnan's literati. The large countertop, crafted from polished inkstone, invites a deeper connection to the material world. Its cool, smooth texture gently registers the temperature of the ingredients. The inkstone's soft surface, responsive to the touch of metal cutlery, produces delicate crystalline chimes—like memories being stirred. On the back wall, an installation inspired by old fish baskets unravels the fragments of daily life and weaves them anew, tracing threads between food, culture, and the essence of living. As Japanese author Tanizaki Jun'ichirō suggests in *In Praise of Shadows*, beauty resides not in the object itself but in the darkness, in the shifting interplay of light and shadow.

As one moves from the Bund into the surrounding neighborhoods, the design of the Hong'anli residential project preserves a more refined side of Shanghai's memory, rooted in the lingering elegance of Jiangnan gardens. Upon entering the foyer, the view extends across the open living room to the courtyard, where lush greenery flows like the spring of Jiangnan. The handcrafted stone wall in the living room, paired with the ink-wash patterned carpet, conjures the poetic imagery of Song dynasty scrolls, evoking the sense of stepping into a living masterpiece. The tearoom, with its tranquil space, invites one to sit by the window, brew tea, and savor its aroma. Behind, jade stone and lacquered screens frame the scene, while calligraphy and a white-glazed teapot rest on the table, exuding timeless beauty. This residence exemplifies the perfect retreat for ancient literati and those who cherish a leisurely life today, where serenity and elegance seamlessly intertwine, leaving a lasting impression. As French priest and scholar Michel de Certeau suggests, memory begins to fade the moment it can no longer be altered or reshaped. Designing a space is an art of bridging memory and reality, where the power of memory lies in its ability to be reshaped, much like our lives, which are constantly intertwined between recollections and progress.

Hai Shang

Shanghai, China – April 2023

Page 150 The circular installation of stacked coastal reeds evokes the rustling breeze of Shanghai's wetlands and memories of childhood water towns. Drawing on Gestalt principles—wholeness, similarity, and continuity—it unites subtle elements into a cohesive form that transcends materiality, awakening collective memory and inviting quiet reflection.

This page The narrow corridor is flanked by textured dark wooden walls, reminiscent of rain-soaked stone walls in a garden. Moss, carefully planted on the stone steps, evokes timeless serenity, guiding one into a poetic, classical world.

This page The paper-mâché lacquer trays for mushroom dishes cleverly blend traditional paper and lacquer craftsmanship. Paired with the inkstone dining counter and metal tableware, they recreate a classic red, black, and silver palette in this modern dining ritual.

Following spread The hand-stacked reed sculpture forms a striking entrance, while the wooden doorplate, inspired by ancient Chinese woodblocks of sacred texts, is skillfully hand-carved.

By the feet, a quiet twist unveils a softly lit aperture, where form gives way to void, echoing the Eastern view of nature, spatial harmony, and the presence of absence.

The black UHPC wall in the dining area mimics the texture of wood grain. The "fish basket"—inspired artwork easily evokes childhood memories of Jiangnan dwellings. Alvar Aalto's "Golden Bell" pendant lights have acquired a patina over time, echoing a simple yet authentic architectural language.

Opposite page The wine cabinet catches the eye. Black bamboo curtains softly drape over the cabinet, offering only a hint of what's inside. Wines from all origins take on an East Asian character here.

This page The large floral arrangement invites guests to reconnect with the sensory experience of being in an Eastern garden, with its fragrant aromas and tranquil visual ambiance, fostering a transcendent dialogue between humans and nature.

Following spread The wide, carved wooden seats and extra-long inkstone countertop create a calm yet inviting atmosphere. The wooden beams on the ceiling, treated with Chinese painting techniques to tone the color, are sourced from reclaimed timber of aged local dwellings. They reflect a respect for materials and convey the spirit of a past era.

THE GRAPHIC WORK
THE WEATHER IS FINE

Hong'anli

Shanghai, China – June 2023

Page 162 Shanghai's heritage also emerges from the tranquil spirit of Jiangnan dwellings. The living room allows generous spacing between furniture and surrounding surfaces. This looseness evokes the calligraphic ideal of *shu ke zou ma* (sparse enough for a horse to pass through). In contrast, books, sculptures, and textured metal panels reflect *mi bu tou feng* (so dense not even wind can pass through). These dualities shape a design as fluid and layered as memory itself.

This page Entering from the foyer, the side tables, coffee table, and sofa mirror the scattered arrangement of tables and benches in ancient Chinese paintings. The wooden sculpture atop the brass-etched table, reminiscent of low garden stones, contrasts with the soaring ceiling above, creating a dynamic and refreshing spatial rhythm.

This page The kitchen flows seamlessly into the living room, forming a serene social space where light and breeze drift through floor-to-ceiling windows that open to the courtyard.

Following spread In the heart of the living room sits my custom-designed "Hai Shang" series sofa. Its moon-white-and-black tones mirror the lacquered coffee table, while an ink-wash carpet beneath suggests the sensation of walking into a painting. The luminous limestone walls, adorned with delicate carvings, recall the grace and sophistication of old Shanghai.

ANDREW MARTIN
TOM FORD

Across from the courtyard, the tearoom catches angled light, casting soft shadows on the jade mosaic screen, as if dawn and dusk quietly share the same space. The lacquered tea table, with bamboo-joint legs, silently echoes the still-life offerings above.

Opposite page A similarly introspective study features bookshelves seemingly carved from the wall. Slender brass accents contrast with the limestone—refined yet warm, modern yet timeless. Handcrafted ceramics add a quiet, rustic touch.

This page The study is awash with soft daylight, exuding the scholarly charm of another time. Whether seated or leaning by the window, one glimpses historic villas nestled in verdant foliage, and everything seems to slow.

Page 172 In the lower-level salon, a metal sculptural display is embedded in the curved oak wall. Precise lighting casts shadows, enhancing the sculpture's mystery. The quiet, restrained atmosphere invites a slower pace, drawing the eye to this miniature stage. In the open bar area, the gray agate-like marble surface mimics ocean waves, while the jade sliding doors act as delicate screens, adding a breath of fresh air to this elegant yet luxurious space.

Page 173 Opposite the sculptural pedestal is a semi-open lounge. A light fabric sofa, faint incense, and a cozy fireplace, paired with a jade coffee table and metal candlesticks, form a private nook for intimate conversation.

BUSINESS LAYOUT
365 Thoughts for Daily Meditation
365 Thoughts for Daily Meditation

A quiet corner of the salon leads to the music room, where light-colored acoustic panels cradle the space in a soft, contemplative hush. The painted screen, with its misty brushstrokes and hues, marks the threshold to a spiritual realm. In the air, the melody of "Aloha 'Oe" lingers, flowing slowly, like shadows gathering at dusk.

The entrance to the music room avoids a direct path, drawing the eye first to a mineral-pigment painting on the right. The figure's calm gaze seems to be listening, or perhaps awaiting the visitor's return. Walls and ceiling in muted wood tones feel quietly expressive. The space evokes a ritual of listening: hushed and reverent, like a courtyard pond whose still surface conceals subtle ripples beneath.

This page A gold-leaf chandelier hangs in the master bedroom foyer, while the sculptural legs of the lacquered round table from my "Hai Shang" series echo calligraphic strokes, fusing stillness with movement and harmonizing modern precision with classical rhythm.

Opposite page Light wood paneling, gold-leaf sliding doors, lacquered furniture, and curated wall art bring harmony to the master bedroom foyer. The mood recalls old Shanghai—a blend of modernity and vintage charm, elegant and poised, with a hint of quiet luxury.

This page A partial view of the master suite. The sliding doors and floor of this suite are handcrafted from Napa leather.

Opposite page A view of the guest suite.

Intended Blank

留

In Eastern landscapes and gardens, emptiness is not nothingness but a space steeped in time, depth, and imagination. Here, both life and space breathe—absence too is a form of abundance.

What can a "blank" do?

Strolling through Ludwig Mies van der Rohe's Barcelona Pavilion, standing before Peter Duesberg's work, or immersing yourself in the silence of John Cage's *4'33"* performance piece, this question might quietly surface. Over the past century, artists have explored the notion of "blankness" through Kazimir Malevich's paintings, Robert Morris's sculptures, Nam June Paik's video art, and others. Whether two-dimensional, three-dimensional, temporal, or sonic, "blankness" has offered profound philosophical meaning and visceral sensory experience. Seemingly empty spaces carry deep emotion and significance, compelling viewers to reconsider the relationship between form and content.

Eastern spatial aesthetics revolve around the concepts of "emptiness" and "tranquility." "Emptiness" is not nothingness but a kind of profound presence—an invisible abundance; "tranquility" is not pure stillness but motion contained within stillness, life pulsing quietly beneath the surface. These ideas are vividly expressed in traditional landscape painting, where delicate brushwork and pale washes dissolve line and form, evoking a vast and boundless realm within the painting. Emptiness becomes a quiet illumination—a Zen state of serene mind and mindful awareness, where pure clarity gently shines within.

In Chinese painting, *liubai* (留白), literally meaning "intentional blank space," emerges as a distinctive compositional technique. Combined with the scattered perspective, it offers viewers multiple vantage points, imbuing the artwork with both spatial depth and temporal rhythm. In a single frame, one often encounters foreground elements—rocks, trees, bridges, and figures—alongside mid-distance landscapes and distant peaks veiled in mist. Here, blankness becomes a connective tissue linking these various visual planes. Like a bird gliding over mountains, this perspective captures intricate details up close while gesturing toward the majesty of far-off scenes. Strategically applied, these blanks allow artists to weave multiple narratives into a single plane, directing the viewer's gaze in a rhythmic dance across space and time. *Liubai* thus transcends the limitations of linear perspective, enabling the viewer to take in the entire landscape while also experiencing a journey through its many parts. Preceding Cubism by centuries, this approach creates a spatial simultaneity—three dimensions on a two-dimensional plane, imbued with a temporal pulse. These intentional blanks also ignite the imagination, inviting viewers to interpret them as clouds, distant lakes, or even transitions between foreground and background. Open-ended and undefined, they suggest endless interpretations. By withholding certain details, the artist guides the viewer to enter the painting—to dream, to complete, to remember. In this way, blankness becomes an art of "less is more," provoking rich imagination with a limited set of elements. It resonates with minimalist design philosophies, where pared-down forms generate emotional and spatial power.

When *liubai* enters the world of modern spatial design, it becomes a language of rhythm and breathability. Seemingly "empty" spaces hold layered emotional and spatial narratives. For example, the Lakeville V residence, which I designed, employs expanses of blankness to evoke a sense of time passing, imbuing the space with a light and breathable atmosphere. Though virtually "blank," the space never feels bare or static. Instead, by drawing on the aesthetic logic of Chinese landscape painting, the design fosters a warm, dynamic spatial experience. Tall potted plants, ink-wash-effect carpets, oversize sofas, and artistically designed ceiling lights emerge as tangible counterpoints to the voids around them. Their forms, textures, and detailing play against the seemingly blank space, composing a black-and-white visual rhythm that opens the space to infinite readings. On the living room's white wall, a frameless ink-washed *xuan* paper art piece settles into its environment with subtlety—its slender form echoing the brush-to-void relationship found in classical painting. The result is a spatial experience of openness, freedom, and quiet unfolding. The room becomes a living scroll—open-ended, contemplative, and charged with emotional resonance. Wherever one stands, there is a moment of quiet anticipation, as though wandering through peaks and streams, waiting for what the next turn will reveal.

Incorporating *liubai,* the design captures the quiet interplay between person and object, fragment and whole. Through absence, it evokes a poetics of presence, materiality, and transience. In such spaces, the external environment meets the inner spirit, conjuring diverse meanings and perceptions. The loosened structure invites deeper spiritual reflection. While conventional boundaries dissolve, consciousness drifts and emotions arise. Rooted in Eastern aesthetic philosophy yet vividly contemporary, *liubai* gives rise to a spatial art that is at once grounded and transcendent—profoundly alive and delicately potent.

A story of cat
ARTS PAPER SECRET
ARTS PAPER SECRET
ARTS PAPER SECRET
ARTS PAPER SECRET
ANDREW MARTIN INTERIOR DESIGN REVIEW

Lakeville V

Shanghai, China – November 2021

Page 184 Eastern art excels at revealing the vast through the minute, and balancing presence with absence. The calligraphy embodies the aesthetics of *liubai*. Dense ink and blank canvas coexist; unpainted areas are not empty but extensions of artistic conception. It is the tension between density and sparsity that shapes the most distinctly Eastern spatial order: not about filling but restraint; not about display but preservation—an aesthetic that invites contemplation and quiet appreciation.

Previous spread The long main sofa, expansive ink-wash carpet, and paper-and-ink installation on the wall echo the vast space beneath the 6-meter-high (nearly 20-foot-high) ceiling—mirroring the interplay of void and form in Chinese landscape paintings. Stepping into the living room feels like entering a painted realm, where scattered perspective gives rise to layered memories that quietly unfold within the seeming emptiness.

Opposite page The unframed artwork by artist Lin Yan, created by layering ink-dyed *xuan* paper, is featured in the space. Its ultra-thin lines engage in a subtle yet powerful dialogue with the surrounding blankness.

This page The artwork on the wall is a metaphor for the space's *liubai*. Through an exquisite contrast of density and sparsity, black and white lines intertwine to form rich textures, conveying a visual tension that is elusive yet powerful, alongside an unhurried rhythm.

Previous spread In Chinese gardens, tall vases bearing large branches evoke a sense of dignity, while single-stem plants such as ferns belong in studies, quiet chambers, or shaded corners of the courtyard. In the living room, greenery of varied scale strikes a balance between expansiveness and poised elegance.

This page From the winding staircase, the view toward the dining and living areas elicits the sense of observing bustle within quietude.

Opposite page The folding doors to the dining room and the elegant marble floor blend the poetic charm of Jiangnan gardens with the refined style of old Shanghai villas.

MODIGLIANI
Christian Parisot
CATALOGUE RAISONNE
世界艺术史
MOREMOREMORE
GIULIO LEONI
HALVBRODERN
TOKYO

Previous spread The staircase's winding form evokes mountain paths in Chinese landscape paintings and the *you shan lang*, covered walkways by water in classical gardens. Below, a modern sculptural stone recalls scholar's rocks, creating a dialogue of movement and stillness. The high-gloss stone floor mimics water and is designed to hold real water if desired, blending poetic symbolism with practical function to evoke a contemplative, serene atmosphere.

Opposite page Within restraint lies richness. The bookshelf, with its slender metal lines, recalls the antique display racks of the Song dynasty. The desk's form evokes the quiet gravity of a traditional scholar's desk, its contours tracing the natural asymmetry of aged timber. Behind it, a dark velvet bed screen, set against minimalist lighting, conjures the spirit of Ming-style furniture: serene, restrained, and timeless.

This page In the study, Ren Tianjin's *Lotus* transcends the flat plane of calligraphy. Through cutting and misaligned reassembly, flowing ink is reimagined as a contemporary spatial language, echoing the room's design rhythm and the nuanced craftsmanship of its furnishings.

Time

時
間

Architecture tames space and shelters the vastness of time. Dwelling becomes the act of turning temporal space into a timeless realm, where one journeys through durée and arrives, in a single breath, at sudden enlightenment.

Modernity begins with the redefinition of time. The invention of the clock extracted humanity from the unhurried, tranquil rhythms of the Middle Ages, thrusting them into a time-space prison meticulously divided into seconds and minutes. The advent of the internet and digital screens has only intensified this acceleration, compressing time into an unrelenting arrow that propels us ceaselessly forward. As a result, space has morphed into a confined box. Charles Baudelaire's lament echoes this transformation: "Time devours life; it takes everything" *(Le Temps mange la vie)*. The essence of twentieth century architecture and art lies in the experience of accelerated time. Structures with immediate visual impact, like skyscrapers, glowing billboards, and glass towers, dominate the urban landscape, while spaces designed for wandering and contemplation, such as Stonehenge or amphitheaters, have grown increasingly scarce. The deep, immersive experience of time has been replaced by the fleeting allure of visual spectacles. In response, designers have sought to reconnect with cultural roots, searching for ways to allow time to unfold, once again, with grace.

In the East, time is intricately woven into the rhythms of nature and life. Spring yields to summer, flowers bloom and fade, and the seasons revolve in a recurring cycle. Chinese paintings often center on "seasonal subjects" such as spring mountains, summer streams, autumn frost, and winter snow. These not only capture the changing seasons but also mirror the shifting moods of the artist. By merging the self with nature, one discovers the essence of life. However, Eastern perceptions of time are not solely cyclical. The Japanese philosophy of *Ichi-go Ichi-e*—that each encounter is unique and unrepeatable—reflects a profound truth: the flowers of summer may return each year, but they are never the same. The ineffable meaning of this concept can only be fully grasped through personal experience. Thus, Eastern time is not confined to monotonous repetition; within the "old," there is always something "new."

In spatial design, time sometimes manifests itself as *durée*. Tool marks left on exposed concrete columns, moss deliberately cultivated on stone steps, or the patina burnished into marble tiles over years of care—all serve as tangible imprints of time. Such details accumulate, forming the texture of a space while imbuing it with vitality. In the restoration and redesign of the Sopher 51 Villa, layers of old paint were intentionally stripped away to reveal fragments of vintage wallpaper from different historical periods. These traces act as temporal slices, exposing nearly a century of history in plain view. Time can also be experienced audibly. In ancient China, literati often retreated deep into the mountains to immerse themselves in the sound of wind through pines. A well-known saying captures this sentiment: “The pine tree, after a thousand years, decays; the mallow flower wilts in one day” (松树千年朽, 槿花一日歇). It illustrates that even a thousand-year-old pine will eventually wither, reminding the Eastern mind not to fixate on preserving the illusion of eternal youth in space through color, form, or symbolism. Instead, they entrust the atmosphere of a space to a single pine tree. Through meticulous pruning and careful care—even replanting pine needles the goal is not merely to replicate the image of pines and cypresses from ancient paintings but to enable the space to listen. It is through this act of listening that the essence of time resonates—not through chronology but as profound presence.

The Eastern view of time, often described as “no longer knowing where it starts or ends,” portrays time as a fluid, boundless force. The Chinese observe the world with an unbroken, flowing perspective—one that transcends the superficial boundaries of time and space. This continuity of experience allows for the transcendence of dualities: the transient and the eternal dissolve into a state beyond time. In spatial design, this sense of wholeness is achieved by relinquishing the desire to impose or overstate, allowing the space to return to its most natural, unadorned essence. As the literati painters have insightfully observed, the distinction between complexity and simplicity lies in the brushwork rather than in the essence of artistic vision.

Space need not be overdecorated, but every detail should evoke warmth and humanity. From hand-polished ceiling moldings to regionally inspired staircases, iron window grills, and furniture imbued with stories, these elements breathe life and authenticity into the environment. A home is the ultimate masterpiece of living—constantly evolving, refining, and redefining itself. This unfolding process requires patience and contemplation, for it is time that imbues space with vitality, enabling it to grow in tandem with its inhabitants. Much like a Chinese garden, a home becomes alive through the delicate movements and transformations brought by time and life, being shaped and reshaped by lived experience. The eternal is but an illusion, Eastern paintings, poetry, and design seek not permanence but transcendence through continuity. Time does not stretch across space; it lingers within it. Space, in turn, awakens through time. In this quiet reciprocity, one finds a profound serenity, where life flows gently, without end or urgency.

Sopher 51 Villa

Shanghai, China – May 2016

DR.

Page 202 Time settles gently into this century-old villa. The stair's handrail, worn smooth by repeated touch, carries the sheen and subtle marks of long-passed years. Faintly visible at the stair's turning point, patterned floor tiles resemble scattered memories, evoking a distant past. Using time as a guiding narrative, the design reveals and refines material textures, allowing natural aging to unfold. In doing so, the space becomes a vessel for history—layered, tangible, and alive.

Previous spread Preserving and adapting architectural details reflects the owner's reverence for the past. In this century-old house, original wall textures remain, while the black-painted staircase brings out time's quiet power through contrast. In the sitting room, a cast-iron fireplace replaced the neglected original, altering the room's sense of scale and its spatial character.

This page A dining room that eases the mind offers more than the warmth of daily meals; it holds a quiet sense of companionship. A long table, half given to flowers, anchors the space, where Roman sculptures murmur of time and greenery softens the stillness. Vintage crystalware and rare Japanese teaware are carefully chosen, each a gentle tribute to beauty, memory, and ritual. There is no rigid division between the dining and the sitting rooms. The eye drifts softly across the threshold, as if thought were gliding from quiet introspection to open conversation, lending the home spatial depth and a quiet intellectual resonance.

Opposite page From the sitting room, the large round mirror on the dining room wall reflects a tranquil scene, like looking through a garden moon gate, deepening the sense of space. The dining room wall, left in its post-paint-removal state, showcases layered vintage wallpaper that resembles slices of time. Each guest leaves their signature, recording time within time.

TATTOO

Collector's Mansion

Shanghai, China – September 2024

Page 208 The Collector's Mansion signifies not only art collections but a timeless archive, blending life and aesthetics in homage to old Shanghai. Curved windows and minimalist design evoke the elegance of Shanghai's early twentieth-century French Concession. Dappled light filters softly through shutters and curtains, while a damaged classical sculpture subtly converses with modern furniture, embodying the city's inclusive spirit. A restrained palette crafts a tranquil, romantic atmosphere that bridges history and modernity.

This page Some say that once you've grown used to walking a certain street, it begins to feel like home. Xiangyang South Road, formerly known as Route Tenant de la Tour, is a place where French villas, garden residences, and Shikumen townhouses quietly coexist. At this site, the building's original structure was retained while refining the façade, carrying forward the spirit of old Shanghai through a careful balance of form, function, and everyday rhythm. Gray terrazzo and pale limestone evoke a shared temperament between Shanghai and Paris—subtle, urbane, and enduring.

At the mansion's entrance, a black-and-white installation composed with precise proportions quietly defines the threshold between residence and street, transforming the urban frontage into a measured passage through space and time. Neither wall nor screen, the half-height structure gently conceals the steps behind it, guiding movement to either side. This subtle detour creates a moment of withdrawal before arrival, shielding the home from the city's clamor while recalling the quiet grace of old Shanghai parlors.

Opposite page The lobby unfolds as a dialogue between classical and modern. Walls clad in Vals stone ground the space with a solemn presence, while the agate-veined marble floor carries the flow of time. At the center of the lintel, an alabaster inlay softly illuminates the path to the elevator hall. It is an object of crystallized emotion, poised between austerity and softness, embodying the rationality and splendor of Europe's Golden Age as well as that of 1920s Shanghai.

This page Each detail resonates, stirring the deepest senses. The inhabitants' first encounter with the building is the door handle of Italian Calacatta marble, which offers a cool, sculptural clarity. A quiet emblem of the "Paris of the East," it bears the gravitas of history and a tactile presence that gently anchors daily life between the tranquil afternoon street and the interior, marking both the prologue to returning home and the first note of refined living.

Previous spread Stepping into the expansive apartment on the second floor, the body is instantly enveloped by soft, diffused light, refreshing air, and a seamless spatial flow. As philosophers Gaston Bachelard and Walter Benjamin have noted, a home is not merely a dwelling but a vessel of time—a place where memories and presence quietly settle.

This page The living room carries a gallery-like monumentality. The concrete display plinth has a raw, unrefined quality, while the antique brass panel behind evokes the oxidized details of historic architecture. The small ceramic piece, with its rough texture, seems unearthed from an ancient ruin. The space inhabits a quiet middle ground, where vintage and modern elements converge, naturally emanating a subdued sense of history.

This page Viewed from the dining room, the kitchen unfolds with quiet clarity. The island anchors the scene, echoing the greenery beyond the window. Warm tones and refined materials create a calm, composed atmosphere.

Following spread Set between repurposed concrete pillars, a low-slung platform sofa faces an 11-by-1.5-meter (36-by-5-foot) terrace, which opens toward the plane-tree-lined streets beyond. Light ivory walls and limestone flooring echo the building's soft beige tones, infusing the space with a calm lucidity. Here, structure yields to atmosphere; the home becomes a contemplative field, where art and everyday life meet.

Pages 220–221 The ideals of nineteenth-century French urbanism have, almost imperceptibly, shaped the temperament of Shanghai's plane-tree-shaded historic district. Absent are grand squares or rigid boulevards, yet the area exudes a relaxed poise—suspended between metropolitan rationality and the meandering spirit of countryside flânerie. In this context, the renovation carries the romantic legacy forward, not through nostalgic revival nor transient trends but through a language of restraint and rhythm that reawakens a life of balance, clarity, and quiet sophistication.

CARPET DESIGN PROJECT OF
TRAVEL ALONG

Kuang-ao

曠奧

Kuang-ao speaks to the ebb and flow of space: *kuang*, expansive and outward; *ao*, inward and hidden. In their alternation, what is concealed draws one in, what is revealed invites one to linger and surrender—together forming a layered rhythm of encounter and reverie.

Humans seek to exist in the midst of change. An open landscape invites one to savor the present moment, while a confined space urges forward motion. Space becomes a mirror of the human soul. Yet, in modern society, whether in structured spaces like hospitals and libraries or open venues like squares and parks, individuals often struggle to feel genuinely present. Existential outsideness seems inevitable. Even when physically within a space, people consciously maintain a distance from their surroundings, feeling displaced and adrift.

Gardens of the Far East, however, offer a contrasting experience—one of delight and engagement. Ancient literati distinguished between the solemnity of temples and palaces, governed by propriety, and the joy of gardens, designed to refresh the spirit and immerse one in tranquility. Garden design emphasizes the interplay of vastness (旷, *kuang*) and profundity (奥, *ao*), alongside the structural harmony of void and substance. Wandering through a garden mirrors the journey of exploring mountains; narrow paths and hidden bridges lead to secluded nooks, while ascents to the rocks and pavilions provide sweeping vistas. The concept of *kuang-ao* (spatial expansiveness and profundity) refers to the dynamic interplay of space opening and closing. *Kuang* represents outward openness, while *ao* symbolizes inward enclosure. These contrasting elements seamlessly blend in garden design, where the skillful transition between exposure and concealment creates an engaging rhythm, offering rich layers and stimulating experiences. The spatial layout of "vastness and profundity" (*kuang-ao*) inherently follows a transition from the confined "profundity" (*ao*) to the expansive "vastness" (*kuang*), mirroring the rhetorical elegance of a periodic sentence. In spatial design, this concept rhythmically orchestrates sensory experiences and emotions, often striking a harmonious balance between intimacy and distance with nature, ultimately cultivating a deep sense of presence.

For instance, in the transformation of an old warehouse into the Weimo Showroom, the original indoor structure was partially demolished and reconstructed. At first glance, the outlines of the spatial volumes resemble the rugged mountain rocks rendered with the "axe-cut strokes" (斧劈皴, *fǔ pī cūn*) in Chinese landscape paintings, emanating a tranquil yet potent energy. The eye is then naturally drawn to the statue placed on a suspended platform—the tall and slender figure resembling a pine tree standing steadfast on jagged mountain ridges. The entire indoor space evokes an immediate impression of a Song dynasty landscape painting.

Passing through a deep, shadowed passage, one enters the café and bookstore on the ground floor, marking the first transition from "profundity" to "vastness." Surrounded by tall, built-in bookshelves, the café evokes a quiet sense of enclosure. Yet from certain angles, the gaze slips through framed openings, meeting the soft greenery of an inner atrium garden and extending toward the rear exhibition hall. Selective removal of the second-floor slab allows light to cascade through the opened voids, casting a soft, natural glow throughout the space. A corridor beside the café gently guides visitors into the exhibition hall, facilitating the second transition from "profundity" to "vastness."

In Chinese landscape painting, hidden mountain paths quietly thread through the terrain. Our team has skillfully translated this element into a sculptural staircase connecting the two exhibition levels. The staircase sides, repurposed from old wooden doors, and the iron railing, subtly colored to reflect the patina of aged wood, evoke a sense of timelessness. Adjacent to the staircase, a display cabinet crafted from similar weathered door panels reveals its mottled hues and traces of decay as one ascends. This natural texture, paired with the elevation change, infuses the space with a raw, unadorned aesthetic. Emerging from the narrow staircase onto the second floor, one is immediately struck by the expansive sensation of vastness. Light pours in from every direction, while only the upper structural supports remain, rendering the second-floor space completely open and airy, akin to reaching a mountaintop plateau after navigating a secluded valley. This completes the third transition from "profundity" to "vastness." Here, visitors linger, rest, read, and appreciate art, savoring moments of serenity suspended in time.

Every journey from "profundity" to "vastness" is, in essence, a philosophical path embodied through movement. Through the spatial interplay of contraction and expansion, the design connects form and spirit. Every winding path and penetrating beam of light quietly narrates the relationship between humanity and nature. In modern society, people often remain distanced from their environment. Yet, the layered transition between "vastness" and "profundity" aptly bridges this gap. Each transition guides individuals inward, reconnecting them with nature and themselves. These spaces, beyond their physical constructs, become shelters for the soul—elicit boundless serenity that transcends the mundane, offering both solace and profound strength.

Weimo Showroom

Shanghai, China – November 2022

Page 226 The Weimo Showroom unfolds through winding transitions, forming layered depths in contrast with moments of openness. This spatial rhythm reflects the organizational logic of Chinese gardens—*kuang* (vastness) and *ao* (seclusion). My saddle-shaped stools mirror this duality: open arches and fluid curves express the expansiveness of *kuang*, while inward-turning surfaces and dense, weighty materiality evoke the introspective depth of *ao*. Sculptural and quietly expressive, the stools resonate with the showroom's spatial rhythm.

This page At the showroom entrance, in the right corner, a cast-in-place concrete sculpture symbolizes the separation and fusion of architectural volumes. Its tactile presence and singular materiality transcend pure visual perception, guiding the aesthetic experience toward an interaction between the artwork and the space. This expression, situated between awareness and environment, responds to the Eastern garden tradition of stone placement in a contemporary manner, while also evoking the site's industrial and suburban historical context.

Opposite page The showroom unfolds like a landscape painting, with varied walls, cantilevered structures, and staircases evincing the "three distances" composition of classical Chinese art. The polished concrete floor suggests a placid lake; staggered volumes recall rocks and pavilions. A sculpture rises in the midground, anchored like a tree emerging from a crag. Above, light spills through perforated planes, drawing the eye upward toward imagined heights and distant realms.

Opposite page The far-left staircase leads to the second-floor showroom, guiding visitors from openness through intimate *ao* to expansive *kuang*. Ground-floor entrances frame interconnecting views like Chinese garden "layered vistas" (透景), also recalling the portals of ancient theaters. The space becomes a quiet stage where restraint and theatricality interplay. Beneath the sculpture pedestal, a semi-enclosed space with bonsai, a Zen lamp, and petrified wood stools echoes classical garden "half-unit" (半间) spaces. Light and shadow mingle here, creating a psychological buffer, an intentional blank.

This page The old factory's roof and beams are preserved, while sections of the floor have been cut or removed, allowing light to pass freely between levels, setting up a spatial drama that plays out across light, levels, and form. Wrapped in burlap, the sculpture dissolves its figurative form, embodying incompleteness and provisionality, and shifting the work toward a more conceptual and emotional register.

This page The ground floor is divided into a front commercial zone and a rear showroom for furniture and art. In the café enclosed by bookshelves, sightlines extend through a lush courtyard to the gallery, or rise via the partially removed floor, forming a vertical dialogue with the upstairs showroom and sculpture plinth. A deep corridor beside the café leads inward, completing a second spatial shift from the intimate *ao* to the expansive *kuang*.

Opposite page In the study-showroom, a tea table inspired by inkstones blends stone and wood textures, imparting scholarly calm to the loosely structured space. Exposed concrete beams and columns; a soft, supportive sofa; and a metal display shelf act as a correlative, their energies weaving a dialogue between nature and artifice, past and present—an essential focus of refined furniture and spatial design.

Page 234 Old door panels are repurposed as staircase sides and wall-mounted cabinets, offering display space for plants and scholars' rocks. The ascent from the first to the second floor becomes another bodily passage—from *ao* to *kuang*.

Page 235 The iron handrails are treated with a metallic finish, giving them a texture and color reminiscent of wood.

Pages 236–237 In the second-floor showroom, intentionally lowered walls open up the view. On the weathered concrete wall, a scroll-shaped sconce quietly conveys the poetic spirit of classical gardens.

Pages 238–239 The Weimo Showroom, located in the suburbs of Shanghai, was originally an old factory.

Sanctuary

聖
所

A sanctuary is not an escape but a spiritual anchor—a renewed gaze of the soul upon the world. Between past and future, the sacred and the mundane, sanctuaries hold the quiet power of calm, allowing us to re-engage with the world more profoundly.

What, then, is a sanctuary? Writer Hilaire Belloc once answered in *The Path to Rome*, "We wander for distraction, but we travel for fulfillment." People long for a sanctuary, seeking to disconnect in order to regain a sense of belonging. A sanctuary is not a complete form of isolation. It offers a unique condition to live: facing the self while also facing nature. A cabin on a cliff or a quiet study in a garden can deepen one's connection with the world. As philosopher Martin Buber said, "All actual life is encounter." The sacred often arises within the "I-thou" relationship, where "thou" can be another person, nature, the world, or even the divine. Design modulates this "encounter." When building a sanctuary by a lakeside or at the edge of a desert, the architecture must hold enough presence to counterbalance the vastness of its surroundings, ensuring it does not shrink into irrelevance in the face of the landscape's grandeur. In mountainous settings, it must respond to the terrain's textures, contours, and layers. Ultimately, the appearance of the sanctuary is a sublime distillation of its locality—a tangible expression of its environment.

Once inside the sanctuary, the interplay between geometry and natural illumination creates a sacred, tranquil atmosphere. Through precise proportions, volume cuts, and the contrast between light and shadow, the space communicates a minimalist yet profound language. Carefully designed openings invite natural light, allowing it to penetrate the space and mark the passage of time. Geometric shapes—squares, rectangles, and orthogonal cuts—when combined with light, transcend mere function, imbuing the space with spiritual symbolism and commemorative significance, transforming it into a place for contemplation and insight. Looking across the space, the sculptural quality and flowing *qi* (vital energy) merge, creating an expression that is serene yet far from cold. The balance between the interior contours and its voids unveils both visual and aesthetic depth. The essence of the design lies not in eliminating excess but in allowing each detail to expand and breathe, so that, within its simplicity, the space becomes rich with depth and dimension. Through the interplay of light and shadow, material choices, and the meticulous handling of spatial forms, the entire space moves beyond the limitations of time and structure, becoming a place where one can deeply connect with one's inner self. The balance between reason and emotion is akin to the peace and awe evoked when facing a snow-capped mountain. For the designer, this is no simple craft.

Different sanctuaries reflect various cultural inspirations for the present day. As an example, take the Deqin Meri Poodom Hotel, designed in the Tibetan region of Yunnan. More than just a temporary resting place for travelers, it functions as a "home," encapsulating the spirit of a different culture. The design not only provides a refuge but also offers a cultural experience. The lobby establishes the first impression. As the door opens, the sound of a cowbell, the warmth of a firepit, and the aroma of butter tea immediately reach the senses, initiating the feeling of being "in Tibet." Outside, the wind and snow are kept at bay, replaced by a breathtaking view of a snow-capped mountain framed by the large window, opposite a soft sofa. The flickering firelight and the coldness of the mountain quietly intertwine in the space, allowing one to experience both the grandeur of nature and the warmth and peace of home. However, the experience within a sanctuary should not be seen as a complete adventure. The exotic scenes and objects, once abstracted and reduced to elemental forms, are reintegrated into the modern space. For instance, the vertical space in the hotel's atrium functions as a conceptual white stupa. The irregular rectangular openings on all four sides, reminiscent of the trapezoidal windows commonly found in Tibetan homes (*tnkhar*), serve as a transition between the harsh plateau climate and human habitation. The restricted view encourages shifts in perspective and moments of pause, turning the act of ascending into a journey toward the inner sanctuary.

The light from the top opening draws the gaze upward. Originally a five-story stairwell, it has been reduced to three stories to maintain a certain distance from the divine light above. The stairwell has been intentionally disconnected from the building's structure in some parts to enhance the sense of fluidity, allowing for a more dynamic interaction with the space. In this dialogue with tradition, modernity gains a new revelation: the sacred mountain remains unconquerable. At the base of the stupa, a body of water reflects the starry sky and the lights at night, with the space naturally "sinking," revealing a touch of ancient mystery. Along the path to the guest rooms, the windows—positioned unusually low—fill the corridor with diffused light, extending the sacred and tranquil atmosphere. Meanwhile, slender black columns punctuate the same corridor like rests in a musical score, breaking visual monotony and guiding the gaze, while preventing awkward, direct lines of sight. The objects within the space carry the traces of time, nurturing the inner senses. The rough warmth of wool felt, the serene black pottery, the slightly cool cast iron, and the stone tabletops—all these tactile objects emit a quiet glow in the cracks of contemporary civilization, inviting one to pause, gaze, and then touch. By integrating into the lives of others, the "retreat sanctuary" becomes, in another sense, a "home."

Between the past and the future, the sacred and the mundane, being in the sanctuary captures the power of calm. People, whether weary or excited, leaving or arriving, experience the potential of these spaces, transforming distant observations into deep participation. The lifestyles and value philosophies of others provide emotional nourishment and spiritual support. Through a window, through a beam of light, the familiar and the distant are connected—sunlight spilling over the golden snow mountains, stars shimmering in the night sky. These secret, meaningful moments help us find our own answers, bridging the distance between the ordinary and the transcendent.

Deqin Meri Poodom

Deqin, China – October 2024

Page 244 The Meri Poodom Hotel's entrance is more than a threshold; it's a narrow gate to a spiritual realm. Stone walls and a wooden door create a solemn, cleansing space. The doorway frames distant snow-capped peaks, mirrored in the waterscape below, extending the view and depth. Rooted in Tibetan materials and mountain reverence, the design evokes a sacred belonging. This warm, otherworldly sanctuary offers an awakening between plateau and city—a true home.

Pages 246–247 In the coldest of places, a massive fireplace soothes weary travelers. The goal of this foyer is not to resemble a traditional hotel lobby, but to evoke a warm Tibetan living room, where firewood and butter tea greet the guests upon arrival.

Page 248 In the public atrium, the white structure defines the space, creating a clear vertical dimension. The rough white paint and openings evoke the purity and energy of Tibetan monastery stupas, bathed in sunlight and silence.

Page 249 Inspired by the varying sizes of the windows of the Tibetan fortress *tnkhar*, the openings invite gazes, glances, and quiet observations. Each aperture becomes a threshold for light and human presence to engage in subtle dialogue.

Pages 250–251 From the lobby, vertical movement begins anew: a 45-degree rotated white stupa replaces the original staircase, forming a sculptural core. Natural light cascades from the skylight above, merging with rays filtered through the wall openings. The boundaries between sacred and profane begin to blur. Visitors can ascend only as far as the third floor—echoing the way one must look up to a sacred mountain, always from a respectful distance.

Pages 252–253 In the second-floor dining room, the cast iron and black natural stone serving counter extends the flavors of the food, creating a visual dialogue with the white stupa. Wooden beams, dining tables, and chairs add warmth, contrasting with the cold outside. The blue-and-white-striped upholstery mirrors the hues of the mountains and sky—a color scheme rooted in Tibetan culture.

Opposite page In the dining area, adjustable lighting adapts to natural light, offering a unique view of the snow-capped mountains in different conditions—whether at dusk, dawn, or on rainy and sunny days.

This page The dining area extends outdoors, offering two panoramic views: one of the snow-capped mountains, the other of the canyon. Spacious sofas, butter-lamp-like candles, and a fireplace create a unique dining experience at 3,600 meters (almost 12,000 feet).

Previous spread In the bar area, the extra-wide window frames the snow-capped mountains like an Eastern scroll painting, contrasting with the warm glow of the fire-place, creating a tranquil atmosphere.

Opposite page The cast iron and textured basalt form the bar's fireplace, creating an old-world ambiance that harmonizes with the experience of enjoying the snow-capped mountains inside the warm interior.

Following spread The private lounge offers snow-capped views on three sides. Low sofas and long tables provide comfort while preserving the intimate feel of a traditional Tibetan living room. In the crisp mountain air, the warmth of butter tea and the steam of Tibetan hotpot create an authentic local dining experience.

Previous spread The offset between the third and fourth floors creates a terracelike viewing platform. A lakelike water feature runs through the space, inviting visitors to walk past it. The displayed sculpture reflects a quiet blessing offered to the Tibetan home.

Opposite page The cabinlike suites perfectly suit the climate of the snow-capped mountains, with their warm textures. The hot tubs and fireplace further enhance this warmth.

Previous spread Vision is key in spatial design. By aligning the angles of the door and windows, a diagonal view is created, allowing guests to continuously glimpse the snow-capped mountains, keeping their majestic presence ever in sight. The serrated textures were intentionally added to the wooden walls, where the humble traces of craftsmanship take on a unique, rare sense of luxury.

Opposite page The terrace, connected to the tearoom, blurs the boundaries between indoors and outdoors. Its open design frames the distant snow-capped mountains, while textured white walls and wooden furniture create a cozy, natural feel.

This page The guest rooms are designed to blend the landscape with the interior experience. Oriented toward the snow-capped mountains, each room is set at an angle to the façade, forming a distinctive triangular outdoor space.

The stone vanity warms in the sunlight, while floor-to-ceiling glass frames the lush mountains. Every corner of the guest room reveals majestic views.

Objects

物

Time, much like the spirit, resists full comprehension. It reveals itself through objects—their shapes, textures, and wear marks bear history's imprint, echoing nature's will and human agency.

Deep in the mountains of southern China, there are villages that have been hidden for centuries. The winds blow gently, the spring water feels cool, and amid the mist stands an ancient Southern Song temple with no Buddhist statues left, silent like a rock. In front of the temple lies a cypress tree, a thousand years old—decaying, withered, as if a gate spanning across time. The architecture here, much like the ancient tree, displays the beauty of the passing of time, accompanied only by moss. Under the eaves, a simple tea bowl epitomizes tranquility across time. The disappearance of an ancient world also carries with it an indescribable vitality. Nothing exquisite remains—only humble, nameless objects, used daily. Who made them? When were they made? Perhaps unimportant.

The German philosopher Oswald Spengler once suggested that humans inherently fear time. This fear, like a mysterious melody, may not be sensed by everyone, but it permeates every true work of art, philosophy, and the formal enactment of meaning. Perhaps it is through humble, unassuming objects that the people of the Far East transform humanity's fear of time into a connection with the ancients, the departed, and oneself. In ancient Eastern cultures, the bond between people and objects ran deep. Even when damaged, cherished belongings were not casually discarded but carefully mended. This gave rise to restoration techniques such as *juci* (锔瓷) and *kintsugi* (金缮). *Juci*, an ancient Chinese technique for repairing porcelain, involved drilling holes on either side of a crack, using curved nails to join the pieces, and applying a special white paste to fill the gaps. For valuable porcelain, metals such as gold and silver were often used for the repair nails. The literati, in their pursuit of natural yet recreated beauty, would intentionally break perfect items and use the repair process to create unique, poetic traces on the porcelain. Japan's *kintsugi* is similar, using vermilion lacquer and gold powder for repairs—revealing rather than hiding, elevating rather than erasing.

Traditionally, attention has often focused on "high art," such as gardens and landscape paintings. Yet, ordinary objects embody the "beauty and authenticity" that could inspire creativity in product design. There's a well-known saying, "Beauty arises from utility." If an object is not frequently used, if it does not feel the warmth of a hand, how can it evoke emotions? Artifacts created by anonymous craftsmen, who may not necessarily be seen as artists, often carry a stronger emotional appeal.

Their beauty lies in frugality and necessity, born from the most primal and unadorned forms and textures. This is evident in the wood-fired pottery of East Asia, where flames freely kiss the ceramic surface, and ash and fire marks bestow warmth and intimacy, sacrificing porcelain's pristine beauty to create a more approachable aesthetic.

At its heart, the inspiration drawn from ancient objects lies in designing with a "pure heart," returning to the pursuit of simple beauty, recognizing the essence of things, honoring nature, and embracing the beauty of imperfection. Design should be approached with genuine spontaneity, adopting a mindset of "no attachment." This allows for liberation from imitating past eras, enabling a direct pursuit of the aesthetic of *gaogu* (高古), or "unadorned antiquity," literally meaning "high antiquity." In merging "unadorned" with "antiquity," it seeks to fade the imprints of time and reality, seeking an artistic depth that bridges past and present, yet remains difficult to mimic.

Objects of "unadorned antiquity" carry a quiet power, displaying a simple yet powerful structure, with a profound, unpretentious essence. They not only demonstrate strength and grace in form but also convey a timeless sense of eternity on a spiritual level. For instance, calligraphy of *gaogu* displays a strong, vigorous stroke with proper form and profound resonance. In short, "unadorned antiquity" does not chase flashy ornamentation but instead reveals an honest, sturdy nature, as seen in the harmonious proportions, precise structures, and flowing lines of the Qingzhou Buddhist statues. This balance between reason and sensibility is the very quality and temperament to be pursued in product design and material development.

As an aesthetic ideal, "unadorned antiquity" arises from reflections on time and space, conveying the transcendent truth through the finite nature of individuals and the fragility of objects. Therefore, Chinese art does not indulge in eternity. Instead, it encapsulates the experience of *gaogu* in every fleeting moment. Much like Eastern wooden architecture, which deteriorates with time and cannot endure like the Gothic cathedrals, it reveals the natural processes of erosion and creation in the flow of time.

When designing products or curating objects, I adore materials such as paper, leather, and bamboo—ephemeral by nature—yet capable of shaping a lasting ambiance within space. These creations convey a sense of liberation and joy—by not defying impermanence and by lending life to space.

My research on paper reflects a contemporary understanding of materials—no longer confined to physical function, but serving as a medium to express ideas, emotions, and philosophy. The core difference from traditional paper lies in its transformation from a mere "tool" to a "language." In this process, paper is not only "used" but also "listened to" and "shaped."

This and opposite page The suspended paper sculpture twists the spatial aura like a "wormhole."

Page 282 Infused with quartz, the dark finishes evoke the effect of transmutation glaze, echoing rocks soaked in mountain rain.

Page 283 Black-glazed ceramic jar, Song dynasty, Northern kiln.

Page 285 Longquan celadon jar with plum green glaze and chrysanthemum petal design, Yuan to Ming dynasties, *juci* (锔瓷) craftmanship.

Page 287 White-glazed stem cup, repaired by gold, Song dynasty; portable African wooden bowl, ca. fifteenth to sixteenth centuries; bowl-shaped yellow pottery from Shaanxi region, Northern dynasties to the Sui dynasty, fifth to seventh century.

Authentic and frugal, ordinary objects reveal a timeless strength and honest spirit through their unadorned forms and materials.

My product designs reflect a pursuit of "unadorned antiquity"—a modern reinterpretation that fuses function with emotional resonance. "The East" is not merely a visual style but a sensibility, imbued with profound philosophical, literary, and sensory significance. It represents the harmonious unity of human and nature, spirit and matter. In the modern era, it is increasingly vital to return to "unadorned antiquity," crafting an artistic vision that connects the past with the present, stirs longing, and remains quietly elusive.

Left The *Yuan* armchair, created in collaboration with the Spanish brand Colección Alexandra, features a curved backrest that naturally follows the curve of the spine. Its structure, made from carbonized ash wood, is inspired by the vigorous strokes of Chinese calligraphy, with its flowing form subtly reflecting the concept of "movement" or "force" in Constructivist art.

Right The floor lamp *Erosion* weaves together interlacing planes to form a sculptural silhouette with an Eastern spirit. Etched metal and irregular lines trace the quiet beauty of imperfection—deliberate, weathered, and serene.

Right The birch wood side table resembles a geometric abstraction of scholar's rocks, combining a sense of modern craftsmanship with the poetic spirit of classical gardens.

The Craft of Shadow Puppetry

Shadow puppetry, originating from the Han dynasty, is said to have been created by Emperor Wu of Han to honor his beloved concubine, Lady Li. Legend has it that artists used animal hides to carve figures and projected their shadows by candlelight to tell stories, marking the birth of this evocative art form. It flourished during the Ming and Qing dynasties and eventually spread to Southeast Asia and Persia via the Silk Road.

The craft of shadow puppetry involves selecting hides, carving, coloring, and assembling. High-quality cow or donkey hides are soaked and polished to create transparent materials. Artisans then meticulously carve the figures, color them with traditional plant-based dyes, and assemble them using strings and bamboo rods for performance.

As one of the world's earliest forms of cinema, shadow puppetry captivated audiences with its vivid storytelling, but it gradually faded from daily life with the rise of modern media, becoming more of a collector's item. I recognized its cultural importance and sought to revive this art form through design projects. The installation pictured on page 293 draws inspiration from the *Classic of Mountains and Seas*, incorporating mythological themes rooted in local history and culture to create a space that resonates emotionally and culturally.

The *Classic of Mountains and Seas* holds deep cultural ties to the Bashu region where the residential project is located. By merging traditional shadow puppetry with modern installation design, I applied perspective techniques from traditional Chinese painting to explore spatial relationships, presenting a cohesive, narrative-driven environment. The large-scale installation stands at the heart of a spacious public area, where light from overhead skylights interacts with shadows, evoking the spirit of Eastern aesthetics.

In the globalized context of art and design, spatial language has grown increasingly homogenized. My modern shadow puppet integrates the "Timeless East" design philosophy with folk art, infusing the space with a strong "spirit of place." Through in-depth exploration of regional culture and contemporary structure, I transcend aesthetic boundaries, emphasizing rationality, practicality, and cultural identity. By deconstructing traditional, cultural, and artisanal elements and drawing inspiration from contemporary art and design, I reintroduced tradition into modern life. In addition to shadow puppetry, I have also conducted in-depth and systematic research on other traditional Eastern materials essential to the spatial experience.

Travelogue on Mountain

Mountain Whispers: Echoes of Deep Time

In the dizzying span of Earth's vast history, time stretches infinitely in both directions from the present. Measured not in minutes or years, but in epochs and aeons, the scale of deep time renders human existence fleeting and minute. Its witnesses are rocks, glaciers, stalactites, seabed sediments, and drifting tectonic plates. Deep time reaches not only into the distant past but forward into an unimaginable future—five billion years hence, when the sun will burn out and the Earth will descend into darkness. This is how Robert Macfarlane, Professor at the University of Cambridge, describes it in his book *Underland: A Deep Time Journey.*

At a moment when the relationship between humanity and nature grows ever more fraught, design is called to adopt a long view—one that draws upon deep-rooted cultural traditions and the intricate interdependence between humans and the world they inhabit. At the thirtieth-anniversary exhibition of Maison&Objet, I responded to the Western academic concept of "deep time," the first work in my *Travelogue on Mountain* series. Through this piece, I explore the evolving relationship between humanity and nature from an Eastern philosophical lens, and imagine a new vitality born at the intersection of tradition and technology.

The installation reinterprets the temporal and spatial language of Chinese landscape painting, rearticulating the idea of nature's eternal presence. It draws inspiration from the Northern Song painter Guo Xi's *Early Spring*, cleverly employing the "rolling-cloud texture stroke" technique (卷云皴, *juǎn yún cūn*) to sculpt a three-dimensional spatial landscape—crafted entirely from paper, the quintessential medium of Chinese landscape art.

As a cultural symbol, paper bears the depth and continuity of Eastern thought, serving as both a quotidian material and a vessel for philosophical expression. I transform this humble material into spatial forms—kneaded, layered, and constructed with quiet precision—to resemble mist, clouds, and mountain ridges. The resulting shapes echo the textured rocks depicted in classical landscape paintings. Paper, fragile and weightless. Clouds, ephemeral. Stones, enduring. This triad of transience and permanence forms a poetic dialectic. The installation also carries a warm, lingering scent of natural materials such as pine soot, resin, and agarwood, all emanating from the ink—a sensory bridge to tradition that invites meditation on the complex entanglement of humanity and nature. Within this paper-formed terrain, intelligent programming simulates the shifting rhythms of natural light, allowing time and space to flow in synchrony.

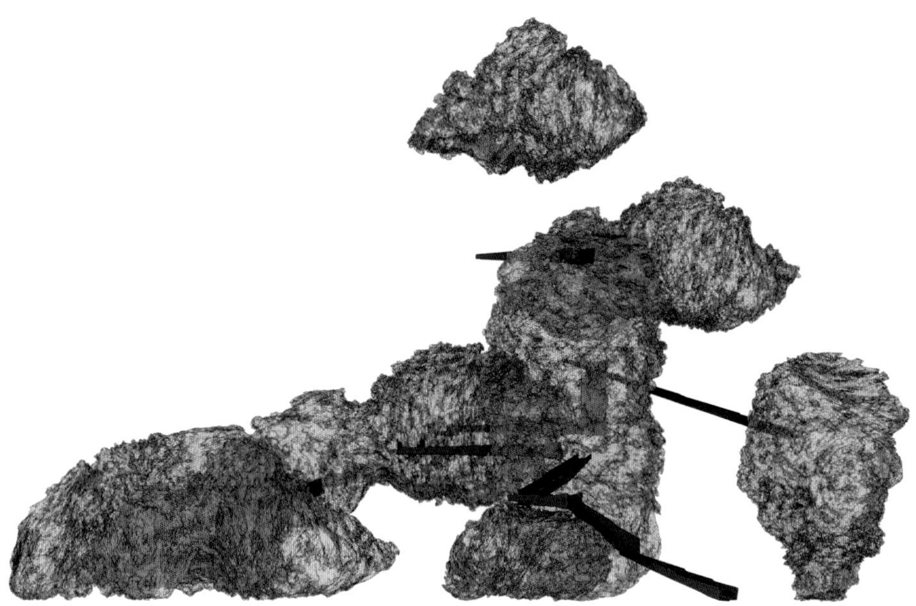

As reality and illusion converge, the installation invokes not only a visual experience but a philosophical reverie.

From afar, metallic structures wrapped in inked paper occasionally pierce through the dark "cloud mountain," resembling mist-veiled paths in ancient paintings or the linear promenades of modern architecture. Up close, paper stones gather discreetly in the corner of the landscape, reminiscent of scholar's rocks in an Eastern garden. Through the seamless fusion of Eastern and Western visual languages and philosophical paradigms, the work meditates on the dualities of impermanence and eternity. Time, in this context, becomes not linear but cyclical and fluid—a passage into inner contemplation.

The "cloud mountain" shifts in layers of light and shadow, where the softness of paper meets the stoicism of stone. Moment and eternity, lightness and weight, ephemeral and enduring—these oppositions form a unique atmospheric tension. The visual and material contrasts provoke reflection on the infinite scope of nature and the brevity of human life, while awakening imagination and a speculative gaze toward the future of time and space. In this Anthropocene era, as human impact becomes geological, how might individual agency be reframed?

Through *Mountain Whispers*, I reimagine "deep time" not solely as geological chronology but as a philosophical meditation on the entangled fate of humans and the Earth. This work embodies a contemporary design ethos—one that is introspective, ecological, and spiritually resonant. With every flicker of light and every shift of shadow, the viewer is drawn into a contemplative journey that transcends time and space.

Pan Yuan: Momentality Unfold

I presented this installation, themed "momentality," at the Milan Design Week 2024. Using paper, a material commonly found in Eastern architecture and painting, the work created a dreamlike Eastern garden experience in the Cortile d'Onore courtyard of the University of Milan. It juxtaposes "lightness and heaviness" and "momentality and eternity" in dialogue with the surrounding historic architecture, echoing the theme of this year's design week, "Cross Vision."

Constructed from lightweight, eco-friendly materials like Dupont paper and aluminum alloy components, the installation stood at the center of the lawn. The viewing experience unfolds in multiple layers: as one walks around the perimeter of the square lawn, maintaining a distance from the installation, the mass and form of its structure becomes apparent. The stacked Dupont paper challenges the usual conventional fragility of paper, giving it a sense of volume. Moving along the path toward the center of the garden, the pure white structure gradually dissolves into gently swaying paper rolls, once again subverting the binary opposition of fragile paper and solid, fixed architecture. Upon entering the installation, glimpses of both the interior and exterior emerge through the gaps between hanging sheets, evoking the sensation of wandering through a dreamlike Eastern garden, where light, nature's scent, bird songs, and the surrounding colonnades create a rhythmically flowing scene.

Pan Yuan is an Eastern garden evolved from Chinese landscape, a space-time entity fragmented into a timeless and temporal existence.

W.DESIGN projects

Sanya Haitang Bay
Pages 22–43
Sanya, China
Completion date: 2023
Area: 4,000m^2 (43,000ft^2)
Design type: VIP club
Developer: China Resources Land (Hainan) Co., Ltd.

The Fame
Pages 48–67
Chengdu, China
Completion date: 2024
Area: 1,200m^2 (13,000ft^2)
Design type: VIP club
Developer: Chengdu Runze Rongcheng Real Estate Development Co., Ltd.

Central Manor
Pages 68–79
Chongqing, China
Completion date: 2022
Area: 1,200m^2 (13,000ft^2)
Design type: VIP club
Developer: China Resources Land Co., Ltd.

Riverside Mansion
Pages 84–101
Hangzhou, China
Completion date: 2022
Area: 530m^2 (5,700ft^2)
Design type: Residence
Developer: Hiwell Properties

Urban Garden
Pages 102–113
Hangzhou, China
Completion date: 2024
Area: 2,100m^2 (22,600ft^2)
Design type: VIP club
Developer: Hangzhou Hepin Real Estate Co., Ltd.
Construction agent: Greentown Real Estate Development Group Co., Ltd.

Domus
Pages 118–133
Shanghai, China
Completion date: 2023
Area: 900m^2 (9,690 ft^2)
Design type: VIP club
Developer: Lonsen Land Group

Arbour
Pages 134–145
Shanghai, China
Completion date: 2024
Area: 400m^2 (4,300ft^2)
Design type: Residence
Developer: China Overseas Land and Investment Ltd.

Hai Shang
Pages 150–161
Shanghai, China
Completion date: 2023
Area: 165m^2 (1,780ft^2)
Design type: Fine dining restaurant
Developer: WS GROUP

Hong'anli
Pages 162–179
Shanghai, China
Completion date: 2023
Area: 600m^2 (6,450ft^2)
Design type: Residence
Developer: China Merchants Shekou Industrial Zone Holdings Co., Ltd., Greentown China Holdings Limited, and Shanghai Land Holdings Limited

Lakeville V
Pages 184–197
Shanghai, China
Completion date: 2021
Area: 650m^2 (6,700ft^2)
Design type: Residence
Developer: Shui On Land Limited
Artwork and floral art: WS SPACE

Sopher 51 Villa
Pages 202–207
Shanghai, China
Completion date: 2016
Area: 330m^2 (3,550ft^2)
Design type: Residence

Collector's Mansion
Pages 208–221
Shanghai, China
Completion date: 2024
Architectural renovation area: 3,860m^2 (41,549ft^2)
Public lobby area: 96m^2 (1,030ft^2)
First-floor residential area: 286m^2 (3,080ft^2)
Second-floor residential area: 450m^2 (4,840ft^2)
Design type: Residence
Architectural renovation: W.DESIGN
Developer: MAISON

Weimo Showroom
Pages 226–239
Shanghai, China
Completion date: 2022
Area: 1,600m^2 (17,200ft^2)
Design type: Exhibition space
Developer: WS GROUP

Deqin Meri Poodom Hotel
Pages 244–271
Deqin, China
Completion date: 2024
Area: 6,000m^2 (64,580ft^2)
Design type: Hotel
Developer: Deqin Meri Poodom Hotel Management Co., Ltd.

Mountain Whispers: Echoes of Deep Time
Pages 294–297
Maison & Objet, Paris, France
Completion date: 2024
Design type: Art installation
Series title: *Travelogue on Mountain*
Medium: Ink on paper

Pan Yuan: Momentality Unfold
Pages 298–299
Milan Design Week, Milan, Italy
Completion date: 2024
Design type: Art installation
Series title: *Travelogue on Mountain*
Medium: DuPont™ Tyvek®, bamboo, and aluminium alloy

Acknowledgments

My heartfelt gratitude goes to my team for journeying through countless moments of creation. Together, we've built a body of work that reflects both depth and diversity.

To every project owner who supported and believed in our design philosophy: thank you. Your trust gave us the freedom to explore, experiment, and ultimately bring these works to life.

I offer special thanks to Catherine Bonifassi and the Rizzoli team for their invaluable guidance and insight throughout the planning and editing of this book.

I am also deeply grateful to the production team—Wang Hang, Shi Dai, Liu Huating, Liu Fangda, and Su Xinxuan—as well as to everyone whose support helped bring this book to completion.

And, finally, I thank myself—for the enduring passion, resilience, and commitment that made it all possible.

Special thanks to our project designers:
Cai Lu, Deng Ting, Dong Yijun, Gao Jiuhong, Gao Yijun, Gao Ying, Gu Xihan, Guo Qing, Hong Yimin, Hu Jingchun, Jia Shan, Lan Ruiyu, Lei Yuqing, Li Qiuyan, Li Xiaoya, Li Yuan, Liu Fangda, Liu Kejun, Liu Yilun, Lu Yingfu, Luo Meng, Mo Haocheng, Qin Jia, Shi Jiaying, Tang Wei, Wang Changhai, Wang Dan, Wang Junchi, Wang Licheng, Wang Lingfei, Wu Jiayue, Wu Shuye, Wu Xianxian, Wu Yin, Wu Yiting, Xu Jingyi, Xu Shuang, Yang Yixi, Yuan Facheng, Yue Shihuan, Zhang Fei, Zhang Kai, Zhang Nianshan, Zhang Shuwen, Zhang Sijing, Zhang Yaping, Zhou Guomei, Zhou Hanyang, Zhou Wei, Zhu Tianliang.

Artistic collaborations

Sanya Haitang Bay

Pages 26–27
Lin Bangde, *Here*, 2023
Rice paper, ink painting (104 x 104 cm; 41 x 41")

Page 39
Su Chang, *Skin Cycle*, 2020
High-strength gypsum, aluminum, hemp, glue (253 x 120 x 95 cm; 99.6 x 47.2 x 37.5")

Riverside Mansion

Page 96
Hu Yiyun, *Derive*, 2022
Ceramics (160 x 130 x 12 cm; 62.9 x 51 x 4.7")

Domus

Pages 118, 120–121
Cat Loray, *The Bride*, 2015
Glazed ceramic, linen string (140 x 103 x 103 cm; 55 x 40.5 x 40.5")

Arbour

Page 134
Shao Lei, *Solidified Interlude*, 2024
Porcelain, plant fiber, pinching, oxidation fired (80 x 100 x 30 cm; 31.5 x 39.3 x 11.8")

Memories

Page 146
You Bo, *Baiyun Nunnery*, 2014
Rice paper, ink painting (70 x 70 cm; 27.5 x 27.5")

Hong'anli

Pages 166–167
Weng Jijun, *Constellation*, 2021
Dry lacquer, malachite green pigment, gold leaves (155 x 144.5 x 10 cm; 61 x 56.8 x 3.9")

Page 172
Zhang Yong, *Watch the Sun*, 2017
Bronze casting (38 x 10 x 5 cm; 15 x 3.9 x 1.9")

Page 173
Du Meng, *Everywhere, Nowhere ll, No.4*, 2019
Glass, multimedia, fabric, silver (17.5 x 20.8 x 9.1 cm; 6.8 x 8 x 3.5")

Page 175
Guan Hailong, *Untitled*, 2021
Rock color (177 x 167 cm; 69.7 x 65.8")

Lakeville V

Pages 184, 197
Ren Tianjin, *Lotus*, 2020
Rice paper, ink painting (200 x 150 cm; 78.7 x 59")

Pages 186–189
Lin Yan, *Passing By*, 2014
Ink, xuan paper (40 x 337 x 5 cm; 15.7 x 132.6 x 2")

Sopher 51 Villa

Page 206
Hiroshi Sugimoto, *Gemsbok*, 1980
Gelatin silver print (42.1 x 54.5 cm; 16.5 x 21.5")

Collector's Mansion

Page 212
Reka Nyari, *Blue Smoke*, 2018
Archival pigment print on acid-free paper

Page 216
Huang Gang, *Loves's Concave*, 2020
Qing yellow glazed tiles, linen, acrylic

Pages 218–219
Wilhelm Sasnal, *Untitled*, 2013
Acrylic on canvas

Pages 218–219
Han Feng, *Bicycle Stadium*, 2015
Acrylic on canvas (200 x 300 cm; 78.7 x 118")

Deqin Meri Poodom Hotel

Pages 246–247
Ryan Mitchell, *Void Flow Bodhisattva*, 2023
Clay with glaze and underglazes (118 x 40 x 35 cm; 46.4 x 15.8 x 13.7")

Page 248
Shao Lei, *Stoneware*, 2023
Pinching, oxidation fired (25 x 25 x 15 cm; 9.8 x 9.8 x 5.9")

Objects

Page 289
Zhang Ruoyu, *The Other Side*, 2013
Bronze (88 x 51 x 37 cm; 34.7 x 20.1 x 14.6")

Page 289
Zhang Ruoyu, *Boy in Shadow*, 2013
Bronze (97 x 51 x 34 cm; 38.2 x 20.1 x 13.4")

Page 290
Ren Tianjin, "溪" (XI)
Detail of calligraphy on xuan paper; exact dimensions unknown

Photography

Timeless East (pages 4–5): Wang Ting
Air (page 18): Sun Jun
Sanya Haitang Bay (pages 22–43): Wang Ting
Enigma (page 44): Shi Dai
The Fame (pages 48–67): Wang Ting, Wang Hang
Central Manor (pages 68–79): Wang Ting
Garden (page 80): Liu Fangda
Riverside Mansion (pages 84–101): Wang Ting
Urban Garden (pages 102–113): Vincent Wu
Nostalgia (page 114): Wang Hang
Domus (pages 118–133): Jerry Chung, Zhu Di
Arbour (pages 134–145): Zhu Di
Hai Shang (pages 150–161): Wang Ting
Hong'anli (pages 162–179): Jerry Chung
Intended Blank (pages 180): Wu Bin
Lakeville V (pages 184–197): Wang Ting
Time (page 198): Shi Zifeng
Sopher 51 Villa (pages 202–207): Jin Xuanmin, Wu Bin
Collector's Mansion (pages 208–221): Howie Zheng, Jonathan Leijonhufvud
Weimo Showroom (pages 226–239): Wang Ting
Deqin Meri Poodom (pages 240–271): Wang Ting
Objects (pages 277–299): Ben Wu, Da Hao, Jerry Chung, Wang Hang, Wang Ting, Shi Dai, Sun Jun

Suppliers

Arclinea, Argile, Asko, Bamboo, Dero, Dornbracht, Ecowater, Empire, Finetouché, Fuli, Gaggenau, Geberit, Gessi, Gira, Hunter Douglas, iGuzzini, Jung, Kallista, Kohler, Leica, Lutron, M77, Moloney, Moorgen, Muli, Neodko, Nocon, Rainwells Group, Reginacasa, Rilang, Sun Joy, Tabu, THG, Vaillant, Verylux, V-ZUG, Yardcom.

Wu Bin
The Design Language of Timeless East

First published in the United States of America in 2026 by
Rizzoli International Publications, Inc.
49 West 27th Street
New York, NY 10001
www.rizzoliusa.com

Text: Wu Bin

Publisher: Charles Miers
Editorial Director: Catherine Bonifassi
Production Director: Maria Pia Gramaglia
Managing Editor: Lynn Scrabis
Copyediting and proofreading: Tricia Levi and Cindy Trickel

Editorial Coordination and Production:
CASSI EDITION
Vanessa Blondel, Ingrid Boeringer, Marie Donzelli, Ilinca Neculcea

ISBN: 978-0-8478-7652-5
Library of Congress Control Number: 2025940851

Printed in China
2026 2027 2028 2029 / 10 9 8 7 6 5 4 3 2 1

The authorized representative in the EU for product safety and compliance is Mondadori Libri S.p.A., via Gian Battista Vico 42, Milan, Italy, 20123
www.mondadori.it

Visit us online:
Instagram.com/RizzoliBooks
Facebook.com/RizzoliNewYork
Youtube.com/user/RizzoliNY

Wu Bin Editorial Team:
Wang Hang, Shi Dai, Liu Huating, Liu Fangda, and Su Xinxuan

www.designerwubin.com
Instagram.com/wubin5
wubindesign@wsdeco.com.cn

W.DESIGN
6F, No.1298, Huaihai Middle Road, Xuhui District
Shanghai, China
www.wdesign.hk
WeChat: wdesign_hk
marketing@wsdeco.com.cn